Cooking Light.

THE Good PANTRY

Cooking Light

THE Good PANTRY

Homemade Foods & Mixes Lower in Sugar, Salt & Fat

OXmoor House®

CONTENTS

Welcome.. 6

Chapter 1: GET READY..8

Chapter 2: CEREAL & BAKING MIXES.....................20

Chapter 3: MAKE-AHEAD DOUGHS.........................58

Chapter 4: DAIRY...114

Chapter 5: JAMS, SPREADS & CONDIMENTS......142

Chapter 6: SNACKS...186

Chapter 7: STOCKS & SAUCES............................238

Nutritional Information..................................264

Metric Equivalents...265

Index...266

WELCOME

Last night I made lentils with sausage and spinach salad for my family. It was a last-minute, off-the-cuff kind of dinner made possible only because my pantry was stocked with the essentials.

Even though my refrigerator was almost empty except for the sausages and spinach, I had fresh garlic and dried herbs to gently fry in extra-virgin olive oil to create the deeply flavored base for the brown lentils. While the lentils simmered and the sausages roasted, I made a dressing by whisking tapenade from a jar with sherry vinegar and olive oil. Call it a pantry dinner on the fly.

A good pantry offers up an arsenal of assertive flavors and flavor-boosting weapons that make your cooking come alive. I'm talking about ingredients like spices and salts, umami-rich flavor bombs like soy sauce and miso, plus a variety of cooking and finishing oils and vinegars. To this, add a bevy of dried whole grains, legumes, and pastas that are easy to keep on hand, and you have the wholesome building blocks in your pantry for any healthy meal.

The contents found in the standard American pantry—packaged, highly processed foods loaded with excess sugar, salt, and trans fats—may provide convenience when your time is in short supply, but they won't make you feel very good. Take inventory: If the labels contain more ingredients than you have fingers, chances are they are full of preservatives. Toss them and start fresh. Start here.

This book gives you the keys to take control of what you feed yourself and your family. So the next time you start your shopping list, open your pantry first, and begin building a better one.

Hunter Lewis, editor of *Cooking Light*

Chapter 1

GET READY

One of the pleasures of a well-stocked pantry (and fridge and freezer) is the ability to put together a meal with minimal fuss. Thaw a ball of made-from-scratch pizza dough, roll it out, top it with the pesto you've made in your food processor, and finish it with homemade mozzarella and a handful of fresh vegetables. Not only does dinner taste delicious, but you've also created a healthy meal that's fresher and better for you than the store-bought or takeout version. Oh, and you've saved a little money, too.

That's the goal behind *The Good Pantry*: to help you create homemade meals using items from your pantry that don't contain the excess sodium and fat or the chemicals and dyes found in many store-bought items. With that in mind, you'll find an assortment of better-for-you versions of popular snack foods, doughs, mixes, stocks, and sauces as well as finished dishes that use those items so you can enjoy the delicious payoffs. You control the ingredients and customize them to suit your tastes using the suggestions you'll find throughout the book or your own flavor preferences. No matter which recipes you try, you'll discover how satisfying it can be to make your own wholesome pantry items.

ABOUT THIS BOOK

Creating your own good pantry doesn't mean you want to spend your weekend in the kitchen, so the recipes in this book are made in small batches. There's no need for hours of chopping and simmering. And for those days when you don't want to, or don't have time to, make everything from scratch, you'll also notice we've included store-bought items that can easily substitute for the homemade versions. Some recipes offer variations to easily change the flavor profile.

You'll also find dietary flags that mark dairy-free, egg-free, nut-free, and gluten-free recipes. Even though peanuts are technically legumes rather than nuts, we've categorized them as nuts for the purposes of this book.

ORGANIZING YOUR PANTRY

Creating a good pantry means getting your kitchen in order. The first step: Take a good look at your cupboard.

◇ **Smell your spices.** Spices are derived from the bark, pods, fruit, root, seeds, or stems of plants and trees. They appeal to our senses, and they're key in healthy cooking. Spices add intrigue, depth, and zest to food without increased calories. They lose their potency after about 6 months. Check the color, too. If it has faded considerably, it might be time to let that spice go.

◇ **Smell your oils, too.** Cooking oils are indispensable. They lubricate food, distribute heat, facilitate browning, create tenderness in baked goods, and provide richness. Many also impart their own unique flavors to dishes. Light, oxygen, and heat cause oils to spoil, so to prolong their life, stash them in tightly sealed, colored-glass or opaque containers in a cool, dark place. Be sure you don't keep them on the windowsill, on the back of your stove, or in a cabinet right above the heat.

◇ **Get organized.** An organized pantry makes meal preparation more organized, too. Put the goods closest to expiration at the front, for high visibility. Create zones for groups of food, such as one for canned beans and vegetables, one for dry mixes, and areas for breakfast and snacks. Place all the Asian ingredients together, if you like, or put the dried shiitake mushrooms in with the vegetables and legumes. There's no one right way to do it.

◇ **Clearly label and date foods.** Properly labeling food can save time and money, and keep your meal plans on track. Nothing derails dinner like finding an ingredient is past its prime. Make sure everything you put into your refrigerator and freezer is clearly labeled and marked with a date. Not all pantry items need a label, such as clear plastic containers of dried pasta or oats. Just mark them with a date to monitor freshness.

◇ **Consider placement to preserve freshness.** A few things you might not know about your fridge: The bottom shelf is the coldest, so store meat, fish, and eggs there. The door is the warmest part of the fridge, so don't store highly perishable items like eggs there. Bottled condiments are perfect in the door.

STOCKING YOUR PANTRY

A functional, well-stocked pantry helps you make a meal without going back out to the store. An ideal pantry contains these items, but feel free to customize this list to your liking and the storage space available.

IN THE PANTRY

◇ **Spices:** caraway seeds, chili powder, cinnamon sticks, ground cinnamon, ground coriander, ground cumin, curry powder, ground ginger, dry mustard, nutmeg, paprika, cayenne pepper, crushed red pepper, and turmeric

◇ **Oils:** extra-virgin olive oil, canola oil, and dark/toasted sesame oil

◇ **Vinegars:** red wine, balsamic, and white. Bonus: apple cider and rice wine

◇ **Seasonings:** lower-sodium soy sauce, salt, black pepper

◇ **Canned and jarred goods:** olives, capers, beans, diced tomatoes, tomato paste, sun-dried tomatoes, pureed pumpkin, tuna, and salmon

◇ All-purpose flour, rolled oats, cornmeal, whole-wheat couscous, baking powder, baking soda, cornstarch, granulated sugar, brown sugar, honey, cocoa powder, chocolate chips, vanilla extract

◇ Dried beans and lentils

◇ Dried pasta

◇ Nuts, seeds, and dried fruit

◇ Potatoes, sweet potatoes, onions, and garlic

ON THE COUNTER

◇ **Fresh seasonal produce:** Watch for ripening, and if you don't think you'll eat within a few days, refrigerate.

IN THE FRIDGE

◇ Eggs, butter, milk, Parmesan cheese, sharp cheddar, lemons, limes, oranges, tahini, whole-wheat flour, ginger, maple syrup

◇ Miso, sambal oelek, Sriracha, canola mayonnaise, Dijon mustard

IN THE FREEZER

◇ Edamame and peas

◇ Chopped spinach, broccoli florets, and corn

◇ Berries

◇ Chicken sausage

◇ Fish

MORE IDEAS

Dry pantry products like pancake and waffle mixes, granolas, and hot drink mixes make wonderful hostess gifts. Put them in Mason jars tied with a ribbon, and include a copy of the recipe. Chutneys, jams, and granolas make great gifts as well. Be sure to mention storage instructions and the expiration date.

SMART SHOPPING TIPS

As tempting as it is when an item goes on sale, most of us don't have unlimited space to buy a truck-load of non-perishables, canned foods, or dry goods. And, it's not much of a savings to buy three bags of flour when you've still got two left a year later. (Flour usually expires before a year.) Here are some pointers for where you can get your money's worth.

KITCHEN TOOLS

Most of the recipes in this book use everyday utensils and pans. Here are a few additional tools you may want to have on hand:

◇ Food processor for quick sauces and dressings
◇ Rolling pin for rolling out dough for piecrusts, pizza crusts, and pasta
◇ Cheesecloth for draining cheese
◇ Thermometer for testing heated milk
◇ Parchment paper for baking
◇ Pizza stone

◇ **Spices:** If you can find a store that sells spices in bulk bins or giant jars, buy only what you need. For most spices, it's much less expensive to buy a tablespoon of, say, marjoram than a whole bottle. Save your old spice bottles and refill them, or buy new glass ones that are all the same size, label them, and store them in a cupboard, away from the light.

◇ **Flours and grains:** Sometimes you only need a little whole-wheat flour, cornmeal, or flaxseed, so buying those from the bulk bins in the grocery store allows you to choose the amount you need. Since whole-grain flours go rancid quickly, it's best to store them in the fridge or freezer. White rice and dried pasta will last a few years in the pantry, but pasta with whole grains has a slightly shorter life span.

◇ **Nuts and seeds:** If nuts and seeds are some of your favorites, buy large amounts and store them in tightly sealed containers in the refrigerator, as shelled nuts can go bad or become stale in a few months if left in the pantry. Keep smaller containers in a cupboard, and refill from your fridge stash as needed. If you need large amounts of nuts for baking or butters, store in double-sealed freezer bags in the freezer.

◇ **Meats, poultry, and seafood:** If you have a big freezer, buy meat, poultry, and fish when they go on sale. It's often less expensive to buy large packages and repackage them into smaller serving sizes that suit your family's needs.

◇ **Produce:** The great thing about buying produce in bulk is that you can do so at the peak of the season, when it's prolific and lowest in price. Some produce, such as beets, potatoes, onions, garlic, and apples, lasts for weeks or even months when bought in bulk, as long as you store them in a cool, dry place, such as a cupboard or basement. Some items look fine but can change in taste over time, such as kale (which becomes bitter) and corn (which loses its natural sugars), so eat them as soon as possible. Mushrooms last longer in paper than plastic.

Keep most produce in the crisper of your fridge. If possible, use one crisper for fruits and one for vegetables to keep gases from building up and causing spoilage. Crispers keep produce items at a higher humidity so they better retain their water and texture, keeping them from drying out. Leafy vegetables and herbs are the most prone to withering, so if your fridge has a crisper you can set for high humidity, stash them there.

SMART FREEZER STORAGE

Part of a good pantry includes quick access to nutritious produce, and one way to get there is to freeze it yourself. Everything from berries, corn, green beans, and peas, to tomatoes and potatoes can be frozen. Whether packing in a plastic bag, jar, or container, leave a half inch for headspace. Without it the water in the produce can make it expand and discolor at the top.

FRUIT

Most fruits freeze well and don't need to be cooked first. Small fruits like berries can be frozen whole. Sweep the fruit into a colander and rinse it quickly. Spread the berries in a single layer on a cookie sheet, leaving some space between them, and freeze until solid. Pack the frozen berries into quart- or gallon-size freezer bags or containers. This flash-freezing process also works well for figs, grapes, sliced pineapple, and rhubarb.

Slice larger fruits into halves or thinner slices. You can also crush or puree them for use as fruit toppings or fillings, or cover the slices with their own juice before freezing. If you love to make pies, make fillings and freeze them, along with piecrust dough, for a winter treat.

An alternative is to freeze fruits in syrup, which preserves their flavor and texture better than flash-freezing but requires more preparation. Peaches need to be blanched and peeled: Make a shallow X on the bottom of each peach. Bring a large pot of water to a boil, and prepare a bowl of ice water. Blanch each peach for 30 to 60 seconds by lowering it into the water in a large slotted spoon. Transfer to the ice water, and peel when cool. Cut each peach into slices. Make a simple syrup using a ratio of 1 cup sugar to 4 cups water. Place the water and sugar in a saucepan, and heat over medium-high heat, stirring until the sugar dissolves. Place the peach slices in a container, and cover with the syrup, leaving ½ inch of headspace. Freeze and use within 8 to 10 months. This process works well with nectarines and apricots, too.

VEGETABLES

When it comes to freezing vegetables, the freshest produce will taste best, so stock your freezer when produce is at its peak. You will need to peel, trim, and cut the produce into pieces first, and blanch them before freezing. Package in plastic freezer bags. Leave ½ inch of headspace, except for asparagus and broccoli.

To freeze corn on the cob, blanch the ears for 7 to 11 minutes, depending on size. Cool completely. Drain and package the corn in plastic bags. To freeze the kernels, stand each blanched cob in a bowl, and slice off the kernels. Package in plastic freezer bags.

Smaller red or gold potatoes are best for freezing, as larger potatoes can become watery when thawed. Boil for 4 to 6 minutes if smaller than 1½ inches in diameter and 8 to 10 minutes if larger. Cool, drain, pack, and freeze. To cook, boil for about 15 minutes.

HERBS

Wondering what to do with the rest of the bunch once you've chopped up the 2 tablespoons herbs required in a recipe? Freeze the rest, and avoid waste and unnecessary expense. The easiest way to freeze herbs is to throw them into a blender or food processor with a little water, and chop. Pour the herb mixture into ice cube trays and freeze; then pop out the cubes, and place them in a zip-top freezer bag. Use the herb cubes in soups, sauces, pasta, and other dishes. You can also put dry herbs on a cookie sheet, and freeze them. Place them in a zip-top plastic bag for later. Frozen herbs are best used for cooked dishes, as they become limp when thawed.

TIPS FOR EFFECTIVE FREEZING

◇ **Use containers that are the right size.** Foods containing liquid can expand, so leave a bit of headspace. Use plastic containers with lids that fit well and seal properly to prevent freezer burn. If you prefer glass, jars work well. Leave 1 inch of headroom, and use only the wide-mouth kind so you can easily get the food in and out.

◇ **Keep food safety in mind.** To prevent bacterial growth, it's important to cool food rapidly so it reaches the safe refrigerator storage temperature of 40° or below. But this can be more difficult with large amounts of food, like soups or large roasts. To speed the process, divide the food into shallow containers or cut large items into smaller portions so they cool more quickly. Hot food can also be placed directly in the fridge or rapidly chilled in an ice-water bath before refrigerating.

◇ **Freeze sauces and soup bags flat.** Pour the cooled mixtures in quart-size freezer bags, and lay them flat so you can easily stack them once they are frozen.

◇ **Utilize ice cube trays.** Freeze stock, chopped herbs, leftover tomato paste, chipotles in adobo, leftover coffee and black tea, and lemon or lime juice in ice cube trays, and then put the cubes in labeled plastic bags.

◇ **Get organized.** This goes without saying, but your freezer is chilly. Keep it organized so you can find things easily when you're pawing through cold containers. Stack anything flat or in a box so you can see the names easily. Create areas for breads, sweets, and meats. Small items fit in door shelves, particularly jars or small bags of coffee or nuts.

◇ **Keep it stocked.** A full freezer is more economical to run because the cold air doesn't need to circulate as much, which requires less electricity to operate.

HOW LONG DOES FOOD LAST?

	PANTRY	FRIDGE	FREEZER
FATTY FISH (LIKE SALMON)		1 DAY	2–3 MONTHS
LEAN FISH (LIKE COD)		1 DAY	6 MONTHS
SOUPS AND STEWS		3–4 DAYS	2–3 MONTHS
COOKED MEAT OR POULTRY		3–4 DAYS	2–6 MONTHS
FRESH POULTRY		1–2 DAYS	9–12 MONTHS
RAW GROUND MEAT		3–4 DAYS	3–4 MONTHS
RAW PORK		1–2 DAYS	4–6 MONTHS
ALL-PURPOSE FLOUR	6–8 MONTHS		
WHOLE-WHEAT FLOUR	1–3 MONTHS	2–6 MONTHS	
WHITE RICE	4–5 YEARS		
BROWN RICE	6 MONTHS		
DRY PASTA	1–2 YEARS		
CORNMEAL	9–12 MONTHS		
RAW EGGS		3–5 WEEKS	
BOILED EGGS IN SHELL		1 WEEK	
BOILED EGGS, PEELED		5 DAYS	
1% OR 2% MILK		1 WEEK	
WHOLE MILK		5–7 DAYS	
BUTTER		3 WEEKS	6–9 MONTHS
HARD CHEESES (LIKE PARMESAN)		2–4 MONTHS	6–9 MONTHS
SEMI HARD CHEESES (LIKE CHEDDAR)		1–2 MONTHS	6–8 MONTHS
FETA		1 WEEK	
CANOLA OIL	2 YEARS		
OLIVE OIL	2–3 YEARS		
PEANUT OIL	3 YEARS		
SESAME OIL	1 YEAR		
VEGETABLE OIL	1 YEAR		
ALMONDS	9–12 MONTHS	1 YEAR	2 YEARS
CASHEWS, PEANUTS	6–9 MONTHS	1 YEAR	2 YEARS
PINE NUTS	1–2 MONTHS	3–4 MONTHS	5–6 MONTHS
WALNUTS	6 MONTHS	1 YEAR	5–6 MONTHS

Chapter 2

CEREAL & BAKING MIXES

Cereal and baking mixes are at the heart of weekend waffles, morning biscuits with butter and jam, and an assortment of sweet and savory muffins and scones. The base mixes for each of these are ideal items to keep stocked in your pantry. They help you get a homemade jump start on some of your favorite baked goods while still leaving plenty of opportunity to customize the flavors to that day's craving.

The base mixes in this chapter are quick to prepare, using some staples you're likely to already have on hand like flour, baking soda, and rolled oats. Unlike packaged mixes, they aren't made with excess sugars or salt and they don't contain any unpronounceable ingredients, artificial flavors, or trans fats. Another perk: They cost less to make than the store-bought options.

Following each mix is a recipe (or two) that employs it, so you can turn a basic biscuit mix into Sweet Potato Biscuits with Honey-Pecan Butter (page 41), or basic muesli into Quinoa-Granola Chocolate Chip Cookies (page 55). You'll find straightforward recipes like buttermilk pancakes that also give you room to experiment with myriad mix-ins for brunch-appropriate items like Gluten-Free Pecan-Oatmeal Waffles (page 34). Or try the variations, which suggest lots of ways to make healthier yet wildly delicious baked goods and cereals.

PANCAKE and WAFFLE MIX

HANDS-ON TIME: 3 MIN. TOTAL TIME: 3 MIN.

This easy-to-make mix comes together so fast you'll wonder why you ever bought the pre-made stuff. With this mix on hand, it's possible to prepare homemade pancakes and waffles on weekdays.

27 ounces all-purpose flour (about 6 cups)
½ cup sugar
2 tablespoons baking powder
2 teaspoons baking soda
1¾ teaspoons salt

1. Weigh or lightly spoon flour into dry measuring cups; level with a knife. Combine flour and remaining ingredients in a large bowl, stirring with a whisk.

Note: This recipe yields 6¾ cups—enough to make four batches of Buttermilk Pancakes. Store in an airtight container in the pantry for up to 6 months.

SERVES 24 (SERVING SIZE: 4½ TABLESPOONS)

CALORIES 135; FAT 0.3G (SAT 0.1G, MONO 0G, POLY 0.1G); PROTEIN 3G; CARB 29G; FIBER 1G; CHOL 0MG; IRON 1MG; SODIUM 386MG; CALC 87MG

buttermilk PANCAKES

HANDS-ON TIME: 15 MIN. TOTAL TIME: 20 MIN.

Fresh buttermilk, the low-fat liquid left after churning butter, helps create light, fluffy pancakes because it reacts with baking soda to prevent the batter from becoming too dense. Small to medium lumps in the batter are fine, but be sure not to overmix, or you'll end up with heavy, tough pancakes. Serve these with maple syrup, honey, jam, powdered sugar, or fresh fruit.

1⅔ cups Pancake and Waffle Mix
1½ cups low-fat buttermilk
1 large egg
1 large egg white

1. Lightly spoon Pancake and Waffle Mix into dry measuring cups; level with a knife. Place mix in a large bowl. Combine buttermilk, egg, and egg white, stirring well with a whisk. Add buttermilk mixture to mix, stirring until smooth. Let batter stand 5 minutes.
2. Pour about ¼ cup batter per pancake onto a hot nonstick griddle or nonstick skillet. Cook 2 to 3 minutes or until tops are covered with bubbles and edges look cooked. Carefully turn pancakes over; cook 1 minute or until bottoms are lightly browned.

SERVES 6 (SERVING SIZE: 2 PANCAKES)

CALORIES 174; FAT 1.7G (SAT 0.7G, MONO 0.5G, POLY 0.3G); PROTEIN 7G; CARB 32G; FIBER 1G; CHOL 33MG; IRON 2MG; SODIUM 472MG; CALC 163MG

VARIATIONS

Fold fresh blueberries, chopped apple, or sliced bananas into the batter.

A few chocolate chips or chopped nuts (walnuts and pecans are tasty options) couldn't hurt. Be sure to toast the nuts before adding them to the batter for the best flavor.

Grated lemon or orange rind adds citrusy interest and flavor. But go easy on those: One teaspoon of rind per 1⅔ cups of the mix is plenty without adding bitterness.

peanut butter and banana
PANCAKES

HANDS-ON TIME: 13 MIN. TOTAL TIME: 13 MIN.

Love banana bread? If so, these are the pancakes for you. Chopped bananas go in the batter, sliced bananas sit on top, and a warm sauce of honey and chunky peanut butter coats it all. Kids of all ages will devour them.

1²/₃ cups Pancake and Waffle Mix (page 23)
¹/₄ teaspoon ground cinnamon
¹/₈ teaspoon ground nutmeg
1¹/₂ cups low-fat buttermilk
1 large egg
1 large egg white
3 medium-sized ripe bananas, divided
6 tablespoons honey
3 tablespoons Peanut Butter (page 160) or natural chunky peanut butter

1. Lightly spoon Pancake and Waffle Mix into dry measuring cups; level with a knife. Place mix, cinnamon, and nutmeg in a large bowl; stir with a whisk. Combine buttermilk, egg, and egg white, stirring well with a whisk. Add buttermilk mixture to mix, stirring until smooth. Chop 2 bananas and fold into batter. Let batter stand 5 minutes.

2. Pour about ¹/₃ cup batter per pancake onto a hot nonstick griddle or nonstick skillet. Cook 2 to 3 minutes or until tops are covered with bubbles and edges look cooked. Carefully turn pancakes over; cook 1 minute or until bottoms are lightly browned.

3. Combine honey and peanut butter in a small saucepan. Cook, stirring constantly, over medium-low heat 3 minutes or until mixture is smooth and thoroughly heated.

4. Cut remaining banana into thin slices. Top pancakes with banana slices and warm peanut sauce.

SERVES 7 (SERVING SIZE: 2 PANCAKES, ABOUT 4 BANANA SLICES, AND ABOUT 4 TEASPOONS PEANUT SAUCE)

CALORIES 283; FAT 5G (SAT 1.2G, MONO 2.1G, POLY 1.3G); PROTEIN 8G; CARB 54G; FIBER 3G; CHOL 29MG; IRON 2MG; SODIUM 439MG; CALC 147MG

VARIATIONS

If you're a peanut butter lover, use this recipe to try other classic combinations: For a take on a perennial favorite, PB&J, skip the banana and add melted jelly to the sauce instead of honey. Or, fold chocolate chips into the batter.

buttermilk Belgian
WAFFLES

HANDS-ON TIME: 20 MIN. TOTAL TIME: 20 MIN.

Dig your waffle iron out of the cupboard for this easy waffle recipe. Egg whites, whipped separately, create air in the batter that makes for tender, high waffles. You can make extra to freeze, and then heat in the toaster to crisp. If you don't have buttermilk, you can make a quick substitute using other dairy products; the texture and flavor won't be quite the same since buttermilk imparts a richness and unique tangy flavor. Use a ratio of 1 cup 2% milk to 1 tablespoon lemon juice or white vinegar, and let the mixture stand 5 to 10 minutes. Or, mix ¾ cup plain fat-free yogurt with ¼ cup water to use in place of 1 cup of buttermilk. These substitutes serve the same purpose, allowing the acid to interact with baking soda or baking powder to aid in leavening.

Cooking spray
1²/₃ cups Pancake and Waffle Mix (page 23)
1½ cups low-fat buttermilk
3 tablespoons canola oil
2 large egg whites

1. Coat a Belgian waffle iron with cooking spray; preheat.
2. Lightly spoon Pancake and Waffle Mix into dry measuring cups; level with a knife. Place mix in a bowl. Combine buttermilk and oil, stirring with a whisk. Make a well in center of mix; add buttermilk mixture, stirring until smooth.
3. Beat egg whites with a mixer at high speed until soft peaks form. Gently fold egg whites into batter. Spoon about ¹/₃ cup batter per 4-inch waffle onto hot waffle iron, spreading batter to edges. Cook 3 to 4 minutes or until steaming stops; repeat procedure with remaining batter.

SERVES 8 (SERVING SIZE: 1 WAFFLE)
CALORIES 170; FAT 5.9G (SAT 0.7G, MONO 3.5G, POLY 1.6G); PROTEIN 5G; CARB 24G; FIBER 1G; CHOL 2MG; IRON 1MG; SODIUM 371MG; CALC 119MG

CITRUSY GINGER-FLAX WAFFLES *with mixed berry compote*

HANDS-ON TIME: 20 MIN. TOTAL TIME: 20 MIN.

These light, lemony waffles and compote, bright with berry flavors, make an indulgent-tasting yet healthy breakfast. As an alternative to the compote, drizzle the waffles with warm honey.

⅓   cup sugar
1   tablespoon cornstarch
1½ cups fresh blackberries
1½ cups fresh blueberries
2   tablespoons fresh lemon juice
Cooking spray
1⅔ cups Pancake and Waffle Mix (page 23)
¼   cup flaxseed meal
1½ cups low-fat buttermilk
3   tablespoons canola oil
1   tablespoon finely grated peeled fresh ginger
1   teaspoon grated lemon rind
2   large egg whites

1. Combine sugar and cornstarch in a medium saucepan, stirring with a whisk to eliminate lumps. Add berries, stirring gently to coat. Add lemon juice. Cook, stirring often, over medium-high heat for 5 minutes or until berries soften slightly and juice is released. Bring to a boil; boil 1 minute or until sauce thickens. Remove from heat; keep warm.

2. Coat a Belgian waffle iron with cooking spray; preheat.

3. Lightly spoon Pancake and Waffle Mix into dry measuring cups; level with a knife. Combine mix and flaxseed meal in a large bowl, stirring well with a whisk. Combine buttermilk and next 3 ingredients (through lemon rind), stirring with a whisk. Add buttermilk mixture to mix, stirring until smooth.

4. Beat egg whites with a mixer on high speed until soft peaks form. Gently fold egg whites into batter.

5. Spoon about ⅓ cup batter per 4-inch waffle onto hot waffle iron, spreading batter to edges. Cook 4 minutes or until steaming stops; repeat procedure with remaining batter. Serve with warm compote.

SERVES 8 (SERVING SIZE: 1 WAFFLE AND ¼ CUP COMPOTE)

CALORIES 254; FAT 7.9G (SAT 1.1G, MONO 1.9G, POLY 4.3G); PROTEIN 6G; CARB 41G; FIBER 4G; CHOL 2MG; IRON 1MG; SODIUM 373MG; CALC 130MG

TECHNIQUE

Properly Peaked

1. Separate the egg whites and allow them to stand at room temperature for 30 minutes. They will beat up higher and faster than egg whites that are cold.

2. Begin by beating with an electric mixer on medium speed until the egg whites curl down when the beaters are lifted out, but the peak almost immediately droops. This is the soft peak stage, which is what we want for waffles, as it makes them fluffy and light as air.

STEP 1

STEP 2

gluten-free oatmeal PANCAKE and WAFFLE MIX

HANDS-ON TIME: 5 MIN. TOTAL TIME: 5 MIN.

- 8 ounces oat flour (about 2 cups)
- 2.1 ounces tapioca flour (about 1/2 cup)
- 5.4 ounces potato starch (about 1 cup)
- 1/4 cup sugar
- 2 tablespoons flaxseed meal
- 1 tablespoon baking powder
- 1 teaspoon baking soda
- 1/4 teaspoon salt
- 1 cup gluten-free old-fashioned rolled oats

1. Weigh or lightly spoon flours and potato starch into dry measuring cups; level with a knife. Combine flours, potato starch, and next 5 ingredients (through salt) in a large bowl, stirring well with a whisk. Add oats, stirring with a whisk.

Note: This recipe yields 5 cups—enough to make two batches of Gluten-Free Oatmeal Pancakes. Store in an airtight container in the pantry for up to 2 months or in the freezer for up to 4 months.

SERVES 20 (SERVING SIZE: 1/4 CUP)
CALORIES 55; FAT 0.8G (SAT 0G, MONO 0.3G, POLY 0.4G); PROTEIN 1G; CARB 11G; FIBER 1G; CHOL 0MG; IRON 0MG; SODIUM 79MG; CALC 28MG

gluten-free OATMEAL PANCAKES

HANDS-ON TIME: 13 MIN. TOTAL TIME: 13 MIN.

These buttermilk pancakes are excellent plain, as the oatmeal adds a wonderful texture (and some fiber, too). You could also spice them up with cinnamon, nutmeg, chopped dried apples, or dried cherries. If you're not avoiding nuts, toasted walnuts are a tasty addition. Top with warm applesauce as an alternative to maple syrup.

- 2 1/2 cups Gluten-Free Oatmeal Pancake and Waffle Mix
- 1 1/2 cups low-fat buttermilk
- 1/4 cup butter, melted
- 2 large egg whites, beaten

1. Place Gluten-Free Oatmeal Pancake and Waffle Mix in a medium bowl. Combine buttermilk, butter, and egg whites; add to mix, stirring until smooth.
2. Pour 1/4 cup batter per pancake onto a hot nonstick griddle or nonstick skillet. Cook 1 to 2 minutes or until tops are covered with bubbles and edges look cooked. Carefully turn pancakes over; cook 1 to 2 minutes or until bottoms are lightly browned.

SERVES 7 (SERVING SIZE: 2 PANCAKES)
CALORIES 242; FAT 9.2G (SAT 4.6G, MONO 2.8G, POLY 1.8G); PROTEIN 7G; CARB 33G; FIBER 3G; CHOL 20MG; IRON 1MG; SODIUM 355MG; CALC 143MG

MORE IDEAS

Serve these pancakes with one of the nut butters on pages 160–163 for a richer meal with more staying power. Heat the nut butter for a few seconds in the microwave to make it easy to drizzle. Top with a little honey.

gluten-free blueberry-almond
OATMEAL PANCAKES

HANDS-ON TIME: 23 MIN. TOTAL TIME: 33 MIN.

These blueberry pancakes get a double dose of almond flavor from the nuts and almond extract. Almond extract can be bitter when used in excess, so don't be tempted to add more. This amount is just right. If fresh blueberries are in season, feel free to substitute them for the frozen called for in the recipe.

2½ cups Gluten-Free Oatmeal Pancake and Waffle Mix (page 31)

1½ cups low-fat buttermilk

¼ cup butter, melted

2 tablespoons maple syrup

¼ teaspoon almond extract

2 large egg whites, beaten

1 cup frozen small blueberries

1 tablespoon oat flour

½ cup sliced almonds, toasted

1¼ cups maple syrup

1. Lightly spoon Gluten-Free Oatmeal Pancake and Waffle Mix into dry measuring cups; level with a knife. Place mix in a large bowl. Combine buttermilk and next 4 ingredients (through egg whites), stirring with a whisk; add to mix, stirring until smooth. Let stand 10 minutes.

2. Combine blueberries and oat flour, tossing to coat. Fold blueberry mixture and almonds into batter.

3. Pour about ¼ cup batter per pancake onto a hot nonstick griddle or nonstick skillet. Cook 2 to 3 minutes or until tops are covered with bubbles and edges look cooked. Carefully turn pancakes over; cook 2 to 3 minutes or until bottoms are lightly browned. Serve with maple syrup.

SERVES 10 (SERVING SIZE: 2 PANCAKES AND 2 TABLESPOONS SYRUP)

CALORIES 319; FAT 8.9G (SAT 3.4G, MONO 3.2G, POLY 1.8G); PROTEIN 6G; CARB 56G; FIBER 3G; CHOL 14MG; IRON 1MG; SODIUM 254MG; CALC 157MG

VARIATIONS

While blueberries and almonds are a classic combination, you could also try chopped apples with toasted walnuts and cinnamon.

For a more sophisticated approach, try chopped fresh apricots with toasted pistachios, or sliced cherries and chocolate chips.

gluten-free
PECAN-OATMEAL WAFFLES

HANDS-ON TIME: 20 MIN. TOTAL TIME: 30 MIN.

Toasted pecans add a nutty sweetness to these oatmeal waffles flavored with cinnamon. Topped with sliced bananas and strawberries and with a swirl of maple syrup for added sweetness, they make a festive, pretty breakfast for your family or brunch for a crowd.

MORE IDEAS

All kinds of fruit have delicious potential as waffle toppings. Beyond fresh berries and banana, try kiwi, mango, or papaya for a burst of color and freshness. Or, sprinkle slices of pineapple with brown sugar or brush them with honey, and then sauté or grill. Pile the warm caramelized pineapple on top of the waffles.

2½ cups Gluten-Free Oatmeal Pancake and Waffle Mix (page 31)
¼ teaspoon ground cinnamon
1½ cups low-fat buttermilk
¼ cup butter, melted
2 tablespoons maple syrup
1 teaspoon vanilla extract
2 large egg whites, beaten
⅓ cup chopped pecans, toasted
Cooking spray
1 cup (⅛-inch-thick) slices banana
1 cup sliced strawberries
½ cup maple syrup

1. Lightly spoon Gluten-Free Oatmeal Pancake and Waffle Mix into dry measuring cups; level with a knife. Combine mix and cinnamon in a large bowl, stirring with a whisk.

Combine buttermilk and next 4 ingredients (through egg whites), stirring with a whisk; add to mix, stirring until smooth. Fold in pecans. Let stand 10 minutes.

2. Coat a round waffle iron with cooking spray; preheat.

3. Spoon about ½ cup batter per waffle onto hot waffle iron, spreading batter to edges. Cook 1½ minutes or until steaming stops; repeat procedure with remaining batter. Top waffles evenly with bananas and strawberries. Serve with syrup.

SERVES 8 (SERVING SIZE: 1 WAFFLE, ⅛ OF FRUIT, AND 1 TABLESPOON SYRUP)

CALORIES 336; FAT 11.7G (SAT 4.4G, MONO 4.2G, POLY 2.1G); PROTEIN 6G; CARB 53G; FIBER 4G; CHOL 17MG; IRON 1MG; SODIUM 315MG; CALC 159MG

BISCUIT MIX

HANDS-ON TIME: 5 MIN. TOTAL TIME: 5 MIN.

Love the idea of whipping up flaky, buttery biscuits on a weekend morning? Speed up the process with this simple biscuit mix that you can prepare ahead and keep on hand. With only four ingredients, not only does it come together quickly, but its simplicity is a plus compared to pre-packaged mixes with unpronounceable ingredients.

45 ounces all-purpose flour (about 10½ cups)
¼ cup baking powder
2 teaspoons salt
1 teaspoon baking soda

1. Weigh or lightly spoon flour into dry measuring cups; level with a knife. Combine flour and remaining ingredients in a large bowl, stirring well with a whisk.

Note: This recipe yields 10¾ cups of mix—enough to make four batches of Buttermilk Biscuits. Store in an airtight container in the pantry for up to 6 months.

SERVES 56 (SERVING SIZE: 3 TABLESPOONS)

CALORIES 85; FAT 0.2G (SAT 0.1G, MONO 0G, POLY 0.1G); PROTEIN 2G; CARB 18G; FIBER 1G; CHOL 0MG; IRON 1MG; SODIUM 201MG; CALC 74MG

buttermilk BISCUITS

HANDS-ON TIME: 5 MIN. TOTAL TIME: 20 MIN.

This rich biscuit recipe comes together easily with our homemade mix. Spreading out the dough rounds on a baking sheet (instead of placing them right next to each other) allows the edges to brown and bake up crisp.

2⅔ cups Biscuit Mix
6 tablespoons chilled butter, cut into pieces
1¼ cups nonfat buttermilk
Cooking spray

1. Preheat oven to 450°.
2. Place Biscuit Mix in a medium bowl; cut in butter with a pastry blender or 2 knives until mixture resembles coarse meal. Add buttermilk; stir just until moist. Pat dough to ¾-inch thickness on a lightly floured surface. Cut with a 2¼-inch biscuit cutter into 14 biscuits.
3. Place on a baking sheet lined with parchment paper. Coat biscuits with cooking spray. Bake at 450° for 13 to 15 minutes or until lightly browned.

Note: If you'd like to freeze these biscuits, prepare the recipe through step 2, and place the raw biscuits on a baking sheet. Cover them with plastic wrap, and place in the freezer. Once they're frozen, transfer to a zip-top plastic bag and freeze for up to 2 months.

SERVES 14 (SERVING SIZE: 1 BISCUIT)

CALORIES 140; FAT 5.3G (SAT 3.2G, MONO 1.4G, POLY 0.3G); PROTEIN 3G; CARB 19G; FIBER 1G; CHOL 14MG; IRON 1MG; SODIUM 267MG; CALC 103MG

MORE IDEAS

Serve these biscuits with a smear of your favorite jam or jelly or a bit of apple butter. Or, try these homemade pantry items: Concord Grape Jam (page 144), Fresh Strawberry Jam (page 147), Apricot-Fig Chutney (page 150), Red Tomato Chutney (page 153), or Quick Gravy (page 246).

herbed asiago BIScUITS

HANDS-ON TIME: 7 MIN. TOTAL TIME: 23 MIN.

Savory additions of cheese and herbs elevate these biscuits to the dinner table. Asiago, a grating cheese, is similar to Parmesan and Romano but not as sharp, and it's friendlier on the pocketbook. If you can't find it, substitute Parmesan, Romano, or a dry Jack. Beyond butter, you could serve these warm and filled with melted cheese, or 1/3-less-fat cream cheese and sliced black olives, or even roasted tomatoes sprinkled with olive oil.

TECHNIQUE

Making the Best Biscuits

1. To make tender, fluffy biscuits, handle the dough as little as possible. Warm hands will cool the butter, which must be kept cold—the cold pockets of butter melt while baking, forming layers of delicious flakiness within the biscuit. Roll the dough around to lightly coat it with flour. Knead just until the dough comes together, about 30 seconds.

2. Pat the dough out lightly to the thickness recommended in the recipe. You'll need to gather the remaining scraps together to make the remaining biscuits. Be sure not to overwork the dough, which can yield tough biscuits.

2²⁄₃ cups Biscuit Mix (page 37)
¼ cup chilled unsalted butter, cut into pieces
3 ounces grated Asiago cheese
2 teaspoons chopped fresh thyme
1 teaspoon chopped fresh oregano
½ teaspoon freshly ground black pepper
1¹⁄₃ cups nonfat buttermilk

1. Preheat oven to 450°.
2. Lightly spoon Biscuit Mix into dry measuring cups; level with a knife. Place mix in a medium bowl; cut in butter with a pastry blender or 2 knives until mixture resembles coarse meal. Stir in cheese and next 3 ingredients (through black pepper). Add buttermilk; stir just until moist.

3. Turn dough out onto a lightly floured surface; knead lightly 5 times. Pat dough to ³⁄₄-inch thickness; cut with a 2¹⁄₄-inch biscuit cutter into 16 biscuits. Place on a baking sheet lined with parchment paper. Bake at 450° for 16 minutes or until lightly browned.

Note: If you'd like to freeze these biscuits, follow the directions on page 37.

SERVES 16 (SERVING SIZE: 1 BISCUIT)
CALORIES 128; FAT 4.6G (SAT 2.8G, MONO 1.2G, POLY 0.3G); PROTEIN 4G; CARB 17G; FIBER 1G; CHOL 13MG; IRON 1MG; SODIUM 262MG; CALC 131MG

STEP 1

STEP 2

SWEET POTATO BISCUITS
with honey-pecan butter

HANDS-ON TIME: 10 MIN. TOTAL TIME: 26 MIN.

Baking a sweet potato brings out its natural sweetness, but if you're short on time, use the microwave instead. Or look for canned mashed sweet potato at specialty markets. Try these split and stuffed with Virginia ham, without the Honey-Pecan Butter.

2²/₃ cups Biscuit Mix (page 37)
2 tablespoons sugar
1 teaspoon ground cinnamon
¹/₃ cup chilled butter, cut into pieces
1 cup nonfat buttermilk
³/₄ cup mashed cooked sweet potato
3 tablespoons softened butter
1 tablespoon honey
¹/₄ cup finely chopped pecans, toasted

1. Preheat oven to 450°.
2. Lightly spoon Biscuit Mix into dry measuring cups; level with a knife. Combine mix, sugar, and cinnamon in a medium bowl, stirring with a whisk. Cut in chilled butter with a pastry blender or 2 knives until mixture resembles coarse meal. Combine buttermilk and sweet potato; add to flour mixture, stirring just until moist. Turn dough out onto a lightly floured surface; knead lightly 5 times. Pat dough to ³/₄-inch thickness. Cut with a 2¹/₄-inch biscuit cutter into 18 biscuits. Place on a baking sheet lined with parchment paper. Bake at 450° for 16 minutes or until lightly browned.

3. Combine softened butter, honey, and pecans in a small bowl. Serve biscuits with butter.

Note: If you'd like to freeze these biscuits, follow the directions on page 37.

SERVES 18 (SERVING SIZE: 1 BISCUIT AND 1 TEASPOON BUTTER MIXTURE)
CALORIES 146; FAT 6.6G (SAT 3.5G, MONO 2G, POLY 0.6G); PROTEIN 3G; CARB 19G; FIBER 1G; CHOL 14MG; IRON 1MG; SODIUM 221MG; CALC 83MG

STEP 1

STEP 2

STEP 3

STEP 4

chocolate-cherry
SCONES

HANDS-ON TIME: 7 MIN. TOTAL TIME: 25 MIN.

These scones use our homemade Biscuit Mix flavored with bittersweet chocolate and dried cherries. Freeze a batch, and reheat by microwaving at HIGH just until warm. Or pop a scone in your toaster oven, and bake at 300° for 10 minutes.

2²/₃ cups Biscuit Mix (page 37)

¼ cup sugar

¼ cup chilled butter, cut into pieces

½ cup dried cherries, chopped

3 ounces bittersweet chocolate, chopped

½ cup nonfat buttermilk

⅓ cup half-and-half

1 large egg

1 tablespoon nonfat buttermilk

2 teaspoons sugar

1. Preheat oven to 425°.
2. Lightly spoon Biscuit Mix into dry measuring cups; level with a knife. Combine mix and ¼ cup sugar in a medium bowl. Cut in butter with a pastry blender or 2 knives until mixture resembles coarse meal. Stir in cherries and chocolate. Combine ½ cup buttermilk, half-and-half, and egg, stirring with a whisk; add to flour mixture, stirring just until moist.
3. Turn dough out onto a lightly floured surface; knead lightly 4 times with floured hands. Divide dough in half. Pat dough into 2 (6-inch) circles on a baking sheet lined with parchment paper. Cut each circle into 8 wedges, cutting into but not through dough. Brush dough with 1 tablespoon buttermilk; sprinkle evenly with 2 teaspoons sugar.
4. Bake at 425° for 18 minutes or until golden. Serve warm.

Note: Store these scones in zip-top bags in the freezer for up to 3 months.

SERVES 16 (SERVING SIZE: 1 SCONE)
CALORIES 178; FAT 6.3G (SAT 3.7G, MONO 1.1G, POLY 0.3G); PROTEIN 4G; CARB 26G; FIBER 1G; CHOL 21MG; IRON 1MG; SODIUM 219MG; CALC 89MG

VARIATIONS

While chocolate and cherry is a heavenly combination, there are others: Try toasted pecans and dried apricots, diced crystallized ginger and lemon zest, or dried cranberries and orange zest.

MUFFIN MIX

HANDS-ON TIME: 3 MIN. TOTAL TIME: 3 MIN.

This mix incorporates whole grains, which enhance the nutrition profile. Be aware, whole grains have a shorter shelf life thanks to the oils they contain, so the mix will last longer if stored in the freezer.

- 22.5 ounces all-purpose flour (about 5 cups)
- 9.5 ounces whole-wheat flour (about 2 cups)
- 2 cups sugar
- 4 teaspoons baking powder
- 4 teaspoons baking soda
- 1 teaspoon salt

1. Weigh or lightly spoon flours into dry measuring cups; level with a knife. Combine flours and remaining ingredients in a large bowl, stirring with a whisk.

Note: This recipe yields 9 cups—enough to make four batches of 12 muffins. Store in an airtight container in the pantry for up to 3 months or in the freezer for up to 6 months.

SERVES 48 (SERVING SIZE: 3 TABLESPOONS)

CALORIES 101; FAT 0.3G (SAT 0G, MONO 0G, POLY 0.1G); PROTEIN 2G; CARB 23G; FIBER 1G; CHOL 0MG; IRON 1MG; SODIUM 191MG; CALC 31MG

blueberry MUFFINS

HANDS-ON TIME: 6 MIN. TOTAL TIME: 33 MIN.

These muffins can be made ahead and frozen. Simply microwave at HIGH for 30 to 45 seconds to warm them.

- 2¼ cups Muffin Mix
- 1 cup low-fat buttermilk
- ¼ cup canola oil
- 1 teaspoon vanilla extract
- 1 large egg
- 1 cup fresh blueberries
- Cooking spray

1. Preheat oven to 400°.
2. Place Muffin Mix in a bowl; make a well in center of mixture. Combine buttermilk and next 3 ingredients; stir well with a whisk. Add to mix, stirring just until moist. Gently fold in blueberries. Spoon batter into 12 muffin cups coated with cooking spray.
3. Bake at 400° for 17 minutes or until muffins spring back when touched lightly in center. Cool in pan 10 minutes. Remove muffins from pans, and place on a wire rack. Serve warm or at room temperature.

Note: Store the muffins in an airtight container in the pantry for up to 2 days, or wrap individually in plastic wrap and store in a zip-top plastic bag in the freezer for up to 1 month.

SERVES 12 (SERVING SIZE: 1 MUFFIN)

CALORIES 167; FAT 5.8G (SAT 0.7G, MONO 3.3G, POLY 1.6G); PROTEIN 3G; CARB 26G; FIBER 1G; CHOL 17MG; IRON 1MG; SODIUM 220MG; CALC 55MG

double chocolate MUFFINS

Cocoa powder provides the deep chocolate flavor of this dessert muffin (although it's certainly a delicious breakfast option, too). If you're a fan of dark chocolate, substitute bittersweet chocolate chips for the semisweet minichips. Notice the secret ingredient? Canned pumpkin creates a moist muffin while keeping the fat in check and without detracting from the intense chocolate flavor.

2¼ cups Muffin Mix (page 44)
¼ cup unsweetened dark cocoa
½ cup semisweet chocolate minichips, divided
1 cup low-fat buttermilk
½ cup canned pumpkin
¼ cup canola oil
1 teaspoon vanilla extract
1 large egg
Cooking spray

1. Preheat oven to 400°.
2. Lightly spoon Muffin Mix into dry measuring cups; level with a knife. Combine muffin mix and cocoa in a medium bowl, stirring with a whisk. Stir in 6 tablespoons chocolate minichips; make a well in center of mixture. Combine buttermilk and next 4 ingredients (through egg), stir well with a whisk. Add to flour mixture, stirring just until moist.
3. Spoon batter into 12 muffin cups coated with cooking spray. Sprinkle batter evenly with 2 tablespoons chocolate minichips.
4. Bake at 400° for 16 minutes or until muffins spring back when touched lightly in center. Cool in pan 10 minutes. Transfer to a wire rack.

Note: Store these muffins in an airtight container in the pantry for up to 2 days, or wrap individually in plastic wrap and store in a zip-top plastic bag in the freezer for up to 1 month.

SERVES 12 (SERVING SIZE: 1 MUFFIN)
CALORIES 204; FAT 8.1G (SAT 2.1G, MONO 4.1G, POLY 1.6G); PROTEIN 4G; CARB 30G; FIBER 2G; CHOL 16MG; IRON 2MG; SODIUM 220MG; CALC 61MG

TECHNIQUE

Making the Best Muffins

1. A good way to avoid overmixing the wet and dry ingredients is to gently fold the ingredients together. Use a spatula to cut down through the center and bring the batter back up to the top. Turn the bowl as you continue folding, to ensure even distribution.

2. The best muffins have a high crown. Baking at a high temperature creates a peak, rather than a domed muffin.

STEP 1

STEP 2

MUESLI
with cranberries and flaxseed

HANDS-ON TIME: 5 MIN. TOTAL TIME: 15 MIN.

Muesli is a popular uncooked cereal composed of grains, dried fruit, nuts, and seeds that have been soaked in milk, fruit juice, or yogurt. This versatile mix is full of heart-healthy fats, whole grains, and seeds. When prepared as a breakfast cereal or added to muffins, it will help keep you full all morning. Store it in the refrigerator to keep the flaxseed and whole grains fresh longer.

- 2 cups old-fashioned rolled oats
- ½ cup sweetened dried cranberries
- ⅓ cup toasted wheat germ
- ⅓ cup ground flaxseed
- 3 tablespoons slivered almonds, toasted
- 3 tablespoons chopped pecans, toasted
- 3 tablespoons pumpkinseed kernels, toasted

1. Combine all ingredients in a large heavy-duty zip-top plastic bag or airtight container.

Note: Store in the refrigerator for up to 6 months.

SERVES 6 (SERVING SIZE: ⅔ CUP)

CALORIES 251; FAT 11.5G (SAT 1.1G, MONO 4.3G, POLY 4.9G); PROTEIN 8G; CARB 33G; FIBER 7G; CHOL 0MG; IRON 2MG; SODIUM 3MG; CALC 17MG

BREAKFAST CEREAL

HANDS-ON TIME: 5 MIN. TOTAL TIME: 3 HR. 5 MIN.

- 4 cups Muesli with Cranberries and Flaxseed
- 3 cups 1% low-fat milk
- ¼ cup maple syrup
- ½ teaspoon vanilla extract
- 1½ cups plain fat-free yogurt (optional)
- 6 teaspoons maple syrup (optional)

1. Combine Muesli with Cranberies and Flaxseed, milk, maple syrup, and vanilla in a large bowl. Cover and chill 3 hours or overnight. Spoon ¾ cup chilled muesli mix into each of 6 bowls. Top each serving with ¼ cup yogurt and 1 teaspoon maple syrup, if desired.

SERVES 6

CALORIES 338; FAT 12.7G (SAT 1.9G, MONO 4.6G, POLY 4.9G); PROTEIN 13G; CARB 48G; FIBER 7G; CHOL 6MG; IRON 2MG; SODIUM 59MG; CALC 183MG

VARIATIONS

Substitute any combination of chopped dried fruit for the cranberries, such as raisins, cherries, apricots, figs, date pieces, or flaked coconut.

Try walnuts or pistachios instead of the pecans, or toasted sunflower seeds instead of the pumpkinseed kernels.

Add rye or wheat flakes, wheat bran, oat bran, or millet instead of the wheat germ.

banana-muesli
MUFFINS

HANDS-ON TIME: 8 MIN. TOTAL TIME: 23 MIN.

These sweet, hearty muffins use two homemade mixes found in this chapter. Cranberries add tart notes, while a little brown sugar and the banana give them sweetness. Extra nutrition comes from the muesli ingredients: wheat germ, oats, seeds, and nuts.

2¼   cups Muffin Mix (page 44)
1½   cups Muesli with Cranberries and Flaxseed (page 49)
¼   cup packed brown sugar
1½   cups low-fat buttermilk
½   cup mashed ripe banana (1 large)
¼   cup canola oil
1   large egg
1   teaspoon vanilla extract
Cooking spray

1. Preheat oven to 400°.
2. Lightly spoon Muffin Mix into dry measuring cups; level with a knife. Combine mix, Muesli with Cranberries and Flaxseed, and brown sugar in a medium bowl; make a well in center of mixture. Combine buttermilk and next 4 ingredients (through vanilla); stir well with a whisk. Add to muesli mixture, stirring just until moist.
3. Spoon batter into 16 muffin cups coated with cooking spray.
4. Bake at 400° for 15 minutes or until muffins spring back when touched lightly in center. Serve warm or at room temperature.

Note: Store in the freezer in zip-top bags (squeeze out air) for up to 3 months.

SERVES 16 (SERVING SIZE: 1 MUFFIN)
CALORIES 178; FAT 6G (SAT 0.7G, MONO 3.1G, POLY 1.8G); PROTEIN 4G; CARB 28G; FIBER 2G; CHOL 13MG; IRON 1MG; SODIUM 175MG; CALC 54MG

nutty whole-grain GRANOLA

✦✦✦✦✦✦✦✦✦✦✦✦✦✦✦✦✦✦✦✦✦✦✦✦✦✦✦✦✦✦✦✦✦✦✦✦

HANDS-ON TIME: 10 MIN. TOTAL TIME: 38 MIN.

✦✦✦✦✦✦✦✦✦✦✦✦✦✦✦✦✦✦✦✦✦✦✦✦✦✦✦✦✦✦✦✦✦✦✦✦

Granola from the grocery aisle is loaded with fats and sugar, and the "light" versions sometimes taste like cardboard. Once you make your own, you'll tamp down the calories and load up on the whole grains, dried fruit, and three kinds of nuts.

✦✦✦✦✦✦✦✦✦✦✦✦✦✦✦✦✦✦✦✦✦✦✦✦✦✦✦✦✦✦✦✦✦✦✦✦

2	cups old-fashioned rolled oats
1	cup packed brown sugar
⅔	cup uncooked millet
⅔	cup dried cherries
¼	cup walnut halves
¼	cup roasted, salted whole almonds
¼	cup hazelnuts
¾	teaspoon kosher salt
3	tablespoons butter, melted
2	tablespoons light-colored corn syrup
1	large egg white

Cooking spray

1. Preheat oven to 400°.
2. Combine first 8 ingredients (through salt), tossing to combine. Combine butter, syrup, and egg white, stirring well. Drizzle butter mixture over oat mixture; toss well to coat.
3. Spread mixture in a single layer on a baking sheet lined with parchment paper coated with cooking spray. Bake at 400° for 27 minutes or until golden, stirring twice. Cool on pan, stirring occasionally.

Note: Store the granola in an airtight container in the pantry for up to 1 month or in the freezer for up to 3 months.

✦✦✦✦✦✦✦✦✦✦✦✦✦✦✦✦✦✦✦✦✦✦✦✦✦✦✦✦✦✦✦✦✦✦✦✦

SERVES 20 (SERVING SIZE: ⅓ CUP)
CALORIES 162; FAT 5.3G (SAT 1.5G, MONO 2G, POLY 1.4G); PROTEIN 3G; CARB 27G; FIBER 2G; CHOL 5MG; IRON 1MG; SODIUM 95MG; CALC 18MG

VARIATIONS

Layer granola, plain yogurt, and berries for a breakfast parfait.

Sprinkle it on top of ice cream.

Top a baked apple or apple pie with granola.

Crumble it on top of muffins for a crunchy finish.

quinoa-granola
CHOCOLATE CHIP COOKIES

HANDS-ON TIME: 25 MIN. TOTAL TIME: 1 HR. 25 MIN.

Satisfy after-school munchies and your dark chocolate cravings with these cookies, made with protein-rich quinoa flour. This recipe uses the Nutty Whole-Grain Granola to amp up the flavor and texture.

4.5 ounces all-purpose flour (about 1 cup)

2 ounces quinoa flour (about ½ cup)

1 teaspoon baking powder

½ teaspoon salt

½ cup granulated sugar

½ cup packed brown sugar

⅓ cup canola oil

2 tablespoons butter, softened

1½ teaspoons vanilla extract

1 large egg

1¾ cups Nutty Whole-Grain Granola (page 52)

⅓ cup semisweet chocolate minichips

1. Weigh or lightly spoon flours into dry measuring cups; level with a knife. Combine flours, baking powder, and salt, stirring with a whisk. Place sugars, oil, and butter in a large bowl; beat with a mixer at medium speed until combined. Add vanilla and egg; beat until well blended. Add flour mixture, beating at low speed just until combined. Stir in Nutty Whole-Grain Granola and chocolate chips. Cover and chill dough 45 minutes.
2. Preheat oven to 350°.
3. Divide dough into 24 equal portions (4 teaspoons each). Roll portions into small balls; arrange balls 2 inches apart on baking sheets lined with parchment paper. Flatten balls slightly. Bake at 350° for 15 minutes or until bottoms of cookies just begin to brown.

Note: Store in an airtight container for up to 5 days.

SERVES 24 (SERVING SIZE: 1 COOKIE)
CALORIES 133; FAT 5.9G (SAT 1.5G, MONO 2.8G, POLY 1.2G); PROTEIN 2G; CARB 19G; FIBER 1G; CHOL 11MG; IRON 1MG; SODIUM 87MG; CALC 20MG

VARIATIONS

Instead of chocolate chips, substitute raisins, shredded coconut, or date pieces.

If you can't find quinoa flour, try brown rice flour. It is close in fiber and binding abilities, but lacks the fat and protein found in quinoa, which is a seed. Brown rice flour is considered a grain.

sunflower
GRANOLA

HANDS-ON TIME: 8 MIN. TOTAL TIME: 16 MIN.

1   cup old-fashioned rolled oats
¼   cup raw sunflower seed kernels
¼   cup shredded sweetened coconut
¼   cup chopped walnuts
¼   cup flaxseed meal
½   teaspoon ground cinnamon
¼   teaspoon salt
2   tablespoons butter, melted
2   tablespoons honey
½   teaspoon vanilla extract

1. Place oven rack about 10 inches below broiler. Preheat broiler to high.
2. Combine first 7 ingredients (through salt) on a baking sheet; toss well. Broil 3 minutes or until lightly toasted, stirring every 1 minute. Combine butter, honey, and vanilla in a small bowl. Drizzle butter mixture over oat mixture; toss to coat. Broil granola an additional 2 minutes or until well toasted, stirring after 1 minute. Remove granola from oven; cool on pan 8 minutes, stirring occasionally.

Note: This recipe yields 2 cups. Store in an airtight container in the pantry for up to 1 week or in the refrigerator for up to 1 month.

SERVES 8 (SERVING SIZE: ¼ CUP)
CALORIES 159; FAT 10.4G (SAT 3.3G, MONO 2.4G, POLY 4G); PROTEIN 4G; CARB 15G; FIBER 3G; CHOL 8MG; IRON 1MG; SODIUM 107MG; CALC 15MG

sunflower granola
BREAKFAST PARFAITS

HANDS-ON TIME: 3 MIN. TOTAL TIME: 3 MIN.

Bust out of your routine with this layered parfait. It takes less than five minutes to assemble, and it's much more fun to look at (and devour) than toast or cereal.

2   cups plain fat-free Greek yogurt
1¼   cups Sunflower Granola
1   cup raspberries

1. Spoon ½ cup yogurt into each of 4 bowls. Top with about ⅓ cup granola and about ¼ cup berries.

SERVES 4
CALORIES 235; FAT 10.6G (SAT 3.3G, MONO 2.5G, POLY 4.1G); PROTEIN 14G; CARB 23G; FIBER 5G; CHOL 8MG; IRON 1MG; SODIUM 150MG; CALC 98MG

VARIATIONS

Try Nutty Whole-Grain Granola (page 52) instead of Sunflower Granola.

Substitute pitted fresh cherries or any ripe berry for the raspberries.

Use sliced bananas and apples, or Mandarin orange segments.

Add a little jam, maple syrup, or honey to plain yogurt for a drop of sweetness.

Chapter 3

MAKE-AHEAD
DOUGHS

Doughs are the foundation of many tasty foods: sweet and savory pies, cheesy breads, pizza, homemade ravioli, corn and flour tortillas. They're also a part of classic dishes from a range of your favorite cuisines, including Steamed Curried Chicken Buns (page 84)—a grab-and-go street food favorite in China—Italian calzones and gnocchi, and American favorites like burgers, doughnuts, and toaster pastries.

If making doughs from scratch is new to you, don't be intimidated. They're easy to prepare, even yeast breads, and you'll find specific guidance in the recipes that follow. The beauty of doughs is that many freeze well, giving you an opportunity to make a big batch to store.

You'll find that these doughs are healthier than store-bought varieties, especially when it comes to saturated fat, sodium, and unwanted additives like dough conditioners. So stock your fridge and freezer with a few of these basic doughs. They'll help you create a healthy, homemade meal easily, even on hurried evenings.

homemade
PIE CRUST

HANDS-ON TIME: 5 MIN. TOTAL TIME: 1 HR. 20 MIN.

Store-bought pie dough is undeniably convenient, but there's satisfaction in making your own. This one comes together so easily you can make several at a time, and then stick the crusts in the freezer. Vodka adds moisture to the dough without the need for added fat. The alcohol bakes off in the oven.

11.25 ounces all-purpose flour (about 2½ cups)
2   tablespoons sugar
1   teaspoon salt
9   tablespoons frozen unsalted butter, cut into small pieces
¼   cup vodka, chilled
¼   cup cold water

1. Weigh or lightly spoon flour into dry measuring cups; level with a knife. Place flour, sugar, and salt in a food processor; pulse 10 times. Add butter, and process until mixture resembles coarse meal. Place food processor bowl and flour mixture in freezer 15 minutes.
2. Place bowl back on processor. Combine vodka and cold water. Add vodka mixture slowly through food chute, pulsing just until combined (do not form a ball). Divide mixture in half. Press each half gently into a 4-inch circle on plastic wrap; cover. Chill at least 1 hour.

Note: This recipe yields 2 pie crusts. To freeze, place the dough wrapped in plastic wrap in a zip-top plastic bag, removing as much air as possible before sealing. Store in the freezer for up to 3 months.

SERVES 20 (¹⁄₁₀ OF ONE PIE CRUST)
CALORIES 112; FAT 5.3G (SAT 3.3G, MONO 1.4G, POLY 0.3G); PROTEIN 2G; CARB 13G; FIBER 0G; CHOL 14MG; IRON 1MG; SODIUM 117MG; CALC 4MG

TECHNIQUE

Making Pie Crust

1. If the chilled pie dough is too stiff, let it sit at room temperature for 5 to 10 minutes before rolling it out. To roll the dough into a circle, apply light pressure while rolling out from the center of the dough. Try to keep the dough thickness even.

2. To flute the pie dough, use two hands to pinch the edge of the crust. Put one hand on the inside edge and one hand on the outside. Push your thumb from one hand between the thumb and index finger of the other hand to form a U or V shape. Continue all the way around the pie plate.

STEP 1

STEP 2

NUT-FREE

EGG-FREE

PEACH PIE
with ginger-pecan streusel

HANDS-ON TIME: 20 MIN. TOTAL TIME: 3 HR. 50 MIN.

Pecans and peaches are a classic Southern combination, and this recipe showcases them both. A double dose of ginger, paired with cinnamon, boosts the flavor of this spiced pie. Bake the pie on the oven's bottom rack to produce a crisp crust.

½   recipe Homemade Pie Crust (page 60)
5   cups sliced peeled ripe peaches
     (2½ pounds)
½   cup granulated sugar
2   tablespoons quick-cooking tapioca
¼   teaspoon ground cinnamon
⅛   teaspoon ground ginger
2.3 ounces all-purpose flour (about ½ cup)
¼   cup packed light brown sugar
⅛   teaspoon salt
3   tablespoons unsalted butter, melted
¼   cup chopped pecans
2   tablespoons chopped crystallized ginger

1. Preheat oven to 400°.
2. Unwrap dough and roll into a 12-inch circle on a lightly floured surface. Fit dough into a 9-inch pie plate. Fold edges under; flute. Line bottom of dough with a piece of foil; arrange pie weights or dried beans on foil. Bake at 400° for 15 minutes or until edge is lightly browned. Remove pie weights and foil; cool crust on a wire rack.
3. Reduce oven temperature to 350°.
4. Combine peaches and next 4 ingredients (through ground ginger) in a medium bowl; let stand 5 minutes. Spoon peach mixture into cooled crust.
5. Weigh or lightly spoon flour into a dry measuring cup; level with a knife. Combine flour, brown sugar, and salt in a small bowl. Add melted butter, stirring until mixture is crumbly. Stir in pecans and crystallized ginger. Sprinkle peach mixture with streusel.
6. Bake at 350° for 1 hour and 10 minutes to 1 hour and 15 minutes or until filling is thick and bubbly and topping is golden, shielding pie with foil if necessary to prevent excessive browning. Cool completely on a wire rack. Cut into wedges.

SERVES 10 (SERVING SIZE: 1 WEDGE)
CALORIES 285; FAT 10.4G (SAT 5.3G, MONO 3.3G, POLY 1G); PROTEIN 3G; CARB 45G; FIBER 2G; CHOL 21MG; IRON 1MG; SODIUM 150MG; CALC 21MG

VARIATIONS

Try this pie with apricots or nectarines instead of peaches, or a mix of all three.

Swap out the ground ginger for ground cardamom for a slightly different flavor profile.

While peaches and pecans are a classic combination, walnuts would work, too.

For the streusel, substitute some of the flour with old-fashioned oats. Doing so boosts the nutrition and lends a nuttier taste.

tomato-ricotta
TART

Make this in the summertime, when heirloom tomatoes and fresh basil are at their peak. The ricotta base is mixed with a bit of Gruyère to amp up the flavor. Just mix up the cheeses, cover with over-lapping tomato slices, and bake.

½   recipe Homemade Pie Crust (page 60)
¾   cup part-skim ricotta cheese or Homemade Ricotta Cheese (page 132)
1   large egg, lightly beaten
2   garlic cloves, minced
½   teaspoon kosher salt
¼   cup chopped fresh basil
1.5   ounces aged Gruyère cheese, shredded and divided (about 6 tablespoons)
1   pound heirloom tomatoes, seeded and cut into ¼-inch-thick slices
Basil leaves (optional)

1. Preheat oven to 400°.
2. Unwrap dough and roll into a 12-inch circle on a lightly floured surface. Fit dough into a 9-inch pie plate. Fold edges under; flute. Line bottom of dough with a piece of foil; arrange pie weights or dried beans on foil. Bake at 400° for 15 minutes or until edge is lightly browned. Remove pie weights and foil; cool on a wire rack.
3. Increase oven temperature to 450°.
4. Combine ricotta, egg, garlic, and salt, stirring with a whisk. Add ¼ cup chopped basil and ¼ cup Gruyère cheese, stirring to combine. Spread ricotta mixture evenly over crust. Arrange tomato slices in a circular pattern over ricotta mixture, slightly overlapping. Sprinkle tomatoes with 2 tablespoons Gruyère cheese. Bake at 450° for 25 minutes or until filling is set. Let stand 10 minutes. Garnish with basil leaves, if desired. Cut into wedges.

SERVES 6 (SERVING SIZE: 1 WEDGE)
CALORIES 296; FAT 17G (SAT 4.6G, MONO 8.9G, POLY 2.5G); PROTEIN 11G; CARB 26G; FIBER 2G; CHOL 48MG; IRON 2MG; SODIUM 340MG; CALC 192MG

VARIATIONS

Instead of the tomato topping, try slices of mushrooms or zucchini strips sprinkled with thyme. You'll want to sauté or roast these vegetables slightly first before using them as a topping to deepen their flavor.

Or fold chopped spinach into the ricotta filling, and top with the tomato slices.

spiced apple
HAND PIES

HANDS-ON TIME: 30 MIN. TOTAL TIME: 2 HR. 9 MIN.

½ cup sugar

¾ teaspoon ground cinnamon

⅛ teaspoon ground cardamom

⅛ teaspoon ground cloves

1½ cups finely chopped Fuji apple

1 recipe Homemade Pie Crust (page 60)

¼ cup all-purpose flour

1 egg, lightly beaten

1. Preheat oven to 425°.
2. Combine sugar and next 3 ingredients in a medium bowl, stirring with a whisk. Reserve 2 tablespoons sugar mixture. Stir apple into remaining sugar mixture in bowl.
3. Divide each circle of dough into 6 equal portions. Working with no more than 3 portions at a time (cover and keep remaining portions chilled), shape each dough portion into a ball; flatten each ball into a 3-inch circle on a lightly floured surface. Roll each into a circle about 5¼ inches in diameter, adding ¼ cup flour as needed to prevent dough from sticking. Trim edges with a 5-inch cutter.
4. Place dough circles on a baking sheet lined with parchment paper. Brush edges of circles with beaten egg. Spoon 2 level tablespoons apple mixture into center of each circle. Fold dough over filling; press edges together with a fork to seal. Brush with beaten egg; sprinkle evenly with reserved sugar mixture.

5. Bake at 425° for 18 to 20 minutes or until golden brown. Cool 10 minutes before serving.

Note: To freeze, place the hand pies in a single layer on a baking sheet after shaping them but before sprinkling with the sugar mixture. Once frozen, transfer them to a zip-top freezer bag, and freeze for up to 3 months. To bake them, place them on a baking sheet, and bake as directed. They may need a few extra minutes in the oven.

SERVES 12 (SERVING SIZE: 1 HAND PIE)

CALORIES 243; FAT 9.4G (SAT 5.5G, MONO 2.4G, POLY 0.5G); PROTEIN 4G; CARB 35G; FIBER 1G; CHOL 38MG; IRON 1MG; SODIUM 202MG; CALC 12MG

Blueberry Hand Pies

Combine 3 tablespoons sugar, 2 teaspoons cornstarch, and ½ teaspoon grated lemon rind in a bowl, stirring with a whisk. Add 1¼ cups fresh blueberries and 1 teaspoon fresh lemon juice; toss well. Roll out, fill, and seal crusts as described in Steps 3 and 4, using 1½ tablespoons blueberry mixture for each pie. Brush with 1 egg, lightly beaten; sprinkle evenly with 2 tablespoons sugar. Bake at 425° for 22 to 24 minutes or until golden brown. Cool 10 minutes before serving.

SERVES 12 (SERVING SIZE: 1 HAND PIE)

CALORIES 223; FAT 9.4G (SAT 5.5G); SODIUM 202MG

strawberry
TOASTER PASTRIES

1   tablespoon water
1   large egg
1   recipe Homemade Pie Crust (page 60)
Cooking spray
$^1\!/_2$ cup strawberry preserves
$^1\!/_4$ cup chopped strawberries
1   teaspoon grated lemon rind
$^1\!/_2$ cup powdered sugar
1   tablespoon strawberry preserves
2   teaspoons fat-free milk

1. Combine 1 tablespoon water and egg in a bowl, stirring with a whisk.
2. Preheat oven to 375°.
3. Working with 1 portion of dough at a time, roll each into a 12-inch square on a lightly floured surface. Cut each into 12 (4 x 3–inch) rectangles. Place 12 rectangles on a baking sheet coated with cooking spray; brush with egg.
4. Combine $^1\!/_2$ cup preserves, strawberries, and rind in a bowl. Spread 1 tablespoon on each of 12 rectangles, leaving a $^1\!/_2$-inch border. Top with remaining 12 rectangles. Press edges together with a fork to seal. Brush pastries with remaining egg mixture. Pierce each several times with a wooden pick.
5. Bake at 375° for 25 minutes or until golden brown. Transfer to a wire rack; cool 15 minutes.
6. Combine powdered sugar, 1 tablespoon strawberry preserves, and milk, stirring with a whisk until smooth. Drizzle glaze over pastries.

Note: These will keep in an airtight container for up to 3 days. Reheat in a toaster or 375° oven for 5 minutes. Or place the pastries in a single layer on a baking sheet and freeze, and then transfer to a zip-top freezer bag for up to 3 months.

SERVES 12 (SERVING SIZE: 1 PASTRY)
CALORIES 252; FAT 9.5G (SAT 5.5G, MONO 2.5G, POLY 0.5G); PROTEIN 3G; CARB 38G; FIBER 1G; CHOL 38MG; IRON 1MG; SODIUM 202MG; CALC 11MG

Cinnamon–Brown Sugar Toaster Pastries with Cinnamon Glaze

Follow directions through Step 3. Combine $^1\!/_2$ cup brown sugar, 2 tablespoons all-purpose flour, and $^1\!/_2$ teaspoon ground cinnamon. Fill and bake pastries as described in Steps 4 and 5. Combine $^1\!/_2$ cup powdered sugar, 2 teaspoons fat-free milk, $^1\!/_2$ teaspoon vanilla extract, and $^1\!/_4$ teaspoon ground cinnamon. Drizzle over pastries.

SERVES 12 (SERVING SIZE: 1 PASTRY)
CALORIES 254; FAT 9.5G (SAT 5.5G); SODIUM 205MG

Fig Toaster Pastries with Lemon Glaze

Follow directions through Step 3. Combine $^1\!/_4$ cup chopped dried figs and boiling water to cover in a bowl. Cover and let stand 15 minutes or until figs are soft; drain. Combine figs and $^1\!/_2$ cup fig preserves in a bowl. Fill and bake pastries as described in Steps 4 and 5. Combine $^1\!/_2$ cup powdered sugar and 1 tablespoon fresh lemon juice in a bowl. Drizzle over pastries.

SERVES 12 (SERVING SIZE: 1 PASTRY)
CALORIES 235; FAT 9.5G (SAT 5.5G); SODIUM 202MG

vanilla
SLICE-AND-BAKE COOKIES

HANDS-ON TIME: 21 MIN. TOTAL TIME: 2 HR. 45 MIN.

9 ounces all-purpose flour (about 2 cups)
1/2 teaspoon baking powder
1/4 teaspoon salt
3/4 cup butter
2/3 cup sugar
1 large egg
1 teaspoon vanilla bean paste

1. Weigh or lightly spoon flour into dry measuring cups; level with a knife. Combine flour, baking powder, and salt. Beat butter and sugar with a mixer at high until light and fluffy. Add egg and vanilla bean paste, beating until well blended. Add flour mixture, beating at low just until combined.
2. Divide dough in half; shape each half into a 4 1/2 x 2–inch log. Wrap logs in plastic wrap, and chill at least 2 hours or up to 1 week.
3. Preheat oven to 350°. Cut each log into 18 (1/4-inch-thick) slices. Place on baking sheets lined with parchment paper. Bake at 350° for 8 to 10 minutes or until edges are lightly browned. Cool completely on a wire rack.

Note: You can also store the logs of dough in the freezer. Wrap them in an extra layer of plastic wrap, and freeze up to 1 month. Thaw in refrigerator before slicing and baking.

SERVES 36 (SERVING SIZE: 1 COOKIE)
CALORIES 84; FAT 4G (SAT 2.5G, MONO 1.1G, POLY 0.2G); PROTEIN 1G; CARB 11G; FIBER 0G; CHOL 15MG; IRON 0MG; SODIUM 58MG; CALC 8MG

Cranberry-Orange Cookies

Prepare dough, adding 1 teaspoon grated orange rind with vanilla. Stir in 2/3 cup chopped sweetened dried cranberries before rolling into 2 (5 x 2–inch) logs; cut each into 20 (1/4-inch-thick) slices.

SERVES 40 (SERVING SIZE: 1 COOKIE)
CALORIES 75; FAT 3.7G (SAT 2.2G); SODIUM 53MG

Spiced Molasses Cookies

Prepare dough, increasing flour to 11.25 ounces (about 2 1/2 cups). Stir 1 teaspoon ground cinnamon, 3/4 teaspoon ground ginger, and 1/4 teaspoon ground cloves into flour mixture. Add 1/4 cup molasses with vanilla. Roll dough into 2 (5 x 2–inch) logs; cut each into 20 (1/4-inch-thick) slices.

SERVES 40 (SERVING SIZE: 1 COOKIE)
CALORIES 81; FAT 3.7G (SAT 2.2G); SODIUM 53MG

Chocolate-Espresso Cookies

Prepare dough, reducing flour to 7.85 ounces (about 1 3/4 cups) and adding 1/2 cup Dutch-processed cocoa and 1 teaspoon espresso powder to flour mixture. Increase sugar to 1 cup. Stir in 3 ounces chopped chocolate before rolling dough into 2 (6 x 2–inch) logs; cut each into 22 (1/4-inch-thick) slices.

SERVES 44 (SERVING SIZE: 1 COOKIE)
CALORIES 87; FAT 4.4G (SAT 2.6G); SODIUM 53MG

homemade
BAKED DOUGHNUTS

HANDS-ON TIME: 8 MIN. TOTAL TIME: 22 MIN.

Make a double batch of these doughnuts, and freeze for effortless weekday breakfasts. Serve slathered with Peanut Butter (page 160) or Chocolate-Hazelnut Spread (page 165).

9   ounces all-purpose flour (about 2 cups)
1   cup sugar
2   teaspoons baking powder
1/2   teaspoon salt
1/4   teaspoon ground cinnamon
1/8   teaspoon ground nutmeg
1   cup 1% low-fat milk
1/4   cup canola oil
1   teaspoon vanilla extract
2   large eggs
Cooking spray

1. Preheat oven to 400°.
2. Weigh or lightly spoon flour into dry measuring cups; level with a knife. Combine flour and next 5 ingredients (through nutmeg), stirring with a whisk. Combine milk and next 3 ingredients (through eggs); add to flour mixture, stirring until smooth.
3. Spoon batter into a large heavy-duty zip-top plastic bag; seal bag. Snip a 3/4-inch hole in 1 corner of bag. Pipe batter into 3 (6-cavity) doughnut pans coated with cooking spray, filling three-fourths full.
4. Bake at 400° for 9 minutes or until doughnuts spring back when touched lightly. Cool in pans 5 minutes on a wire rack. Transfer doughnuts to a wire rack.

Note: To freeze, place glazed or unglazed doughnuts in a large heavy-duty zip-top plastic bag. Seal bag, and freeze up to 2 weeks. To thaw, let stand, uncovered, at room temperature 40 minutes.

SERVES 18 (SERVING SIZE: 1 DOUGHNUT)
CALORIES 139; FAT 4.1G (SAT 0.6G, MONO 1.7G, POLY 1.5G); PROTEIN 3G; CARB 23G; FIBER 0G; CHOL 21MG; IRON 1MG; SODIUM 129MG; CALC 59MG

Chocolate-Glazed Doughnuts

Place 1/4 cup 1% low-fat milk in a medium microwave-safe bowl. Microwave at HIGH 1 minute. Add 1 cup semisweet chocolate chips; stir 30 seconds or until smooth. Gradually add 1/2 cup powdered sugar, stirring until smooth. Dip tops of doughnuts in glaze, allowing excess to drip into bowl. Place doughnuts, glazed side up, on a wire rack; let stand until glaze is set.

SERVES 18 (SERVING SIZE: 1 DOUGHNUT)
CALORIES 198; FAT 6.9G (SAT 2.3G); SODIUM 132MG

Cinnamon-Glazed Doughnuts

Combine 2 cups powdered sugar, 1/3 cup boiling water, and 1/4 teaspoon ground cinnamon in a small bowl, stirring until smooth. Dip tops of doughnuts in glaze, allowing excess to drip into bowl. Place doughnuts, glazed side up, on a wire rack; let stand until glaze is set.

SERVES 18 (SERVING SIZE: 1 DOUGHNUT)
CALORIES 191; FAT 4.1G (SAT 0.6G); SODIUM 129MG

CINNAMON ROLLS
with dates

HANDS-ON TIME: 25 MIN. TOTAL TIME: 2 HR. 34 MIN.

2   packages dry yeast (about 4½ teaspoons)
¾   cup warm unsweetened vanilla almond milk (100° to 110°)
¼   cup warm water (100° to 110°)
9   ounces all-purpose flour (about 2 cups)
7.1 ounces whole-wheat flour (about 1½ cups)
¼   cup butter, softened
¼   cup honey
½   teaspoon salt
1½ teaspoons orange juice
1   large egg, beaten
1   large egg white, beaten
    Cooking spray
½   cup whole pitted Medjool dates (8 dates)
½   cup boiling water
¼   cup packed brown sugar
1   tablespoon ground cinnamon
¼   teaspoon ground cardamom
½   cup currants
1   cup powdered sugar, sifted
¾   teaspoon vanilla extract
4   teaspoons unsweetened vanilla almond milk

1. Combine first 3 ingredients in a large bowl, stirring to dissolve yeast; let stand 5 minutes. Weigh or lightly spoon flours into dry measuring cups; level with a knife. Add flours and next 6 ingredients (through egg white) to yeast mixture, stirring until a soft dough forms.
2. Turn dough out onto a floured surface. Knead until smooth and elastic (about 4 minutes). Place dough in a large bowl coated with cooking spray, turning to coat top. Cover and let rise in a warm place (85°), free from drafts, 1 hour or until doubled in size. (Gently press two fingers into dough. If indentation remains, dough has risen enough.) Punch dough down; roll into a 16 x 12–inch rectangle on a floured surface. Coat surface of dough with cooking spray.
3. Place dates and boiling water in a bowl; let stand 5 minutes. Place date mixture in a food processor; pulse 5 times or until a paste forms. Add brown sugar, cinnamon, and cardamom; pulse 1 to 2 times or until blended.
4. Spread filling over dough, leaving a ½-inch border. Sprinkle currants over filling, pressing gently into filling. Roll up rectangle tightly, starting with a long edge, pressing firmly to eliminate air pockets; pinch seam to seal. Cut roll into 16 slices. Place slices, cut sides up, in a 13 x 9–inch metal baking pan coated with cooking spray. Cover and let rise 35 to 40 minutes or until doubled in size.
5. Preheat oven to 375°.
6. Bake at 375° for 19 minutes or until lightly browned. Cool in pan on a wire rack.
7. Place powdered sugar and vanilla in a small bowl. Add 4 teaspoons almond milk, 1 teaspoon at a time, stirring to form a thick glaze. Drizzle glaze evenly over rolls.

SERVES 16 (SERVING SIZE: 1 ROLL)
CALORIES 230; FAT 4G (SAT 2G, MONO 1.1G, POLY 0.4G); PROTEIN 5G; CARB 46G; FIBER 3G; CHOL 19MG; IRON 2MG; SODIUM 118MG; CALC 49MG

VARIATIONS

Instead of a glaze, top the cinnamon rolls with caramel sauce.

When it comes time to roll up the dough, add a layer of fresh blueberries, raisins, or chocolate chips.

Top the buns with chopped roasted pecans or walnuts to add a little crunch.

PIZZA DOUGH

HANDS-ON TIME: 15 MIN. TOTAL TIME: 25 HR. 15 MIN.

1   package dry yeast (about 2½ teaspoons)
⅔   cup warm water (100° to 110°)
1   cup cold water
1½   tablespoons olive oil
18   ounces unbleached bread flour (about 4 cups), divided
¾   teaspoon sugar
¾   teaspoon salt
Cooking spray

1. Dissolve yeast in ⅔ cup warm water in the bowl of a stand mixer; let stand 5 minutes. Stir in 1 cup cold water and oil.
2. Weigh or lightly spoon flour into dry measuring cups; level with a knife. Gradually add 9 ounces flour (about 2 cups), sugar, and salt to yeast mixture; beat at low speed until smooth. Gradually add 7.9 ounces flour (about 1¾ cups); beat until smooth. Turn dough out onto a floured surface. Knead until smooth and elastic (about 10 minutes); add enough of remaining flour, 1 tablespoon at a time, to prevent dough from sticking to hands (dough will feel sticky).
3. Divide dough in half; shape each half into a ball. Place each portion in a zip-top plastic bag coated with cooking spray. Seal. Chill overnight or up to 2 days. Let stand at room temperature 1 hour before using.

Note: This recipes makes 2 (1-pound) balls of dough. Store it the freezer for up to 3 months, and then thaw overnight.

SERVES 16

CALORIES 129; FAT 1.9G (SAT 0.3G, MONO 1G, POLY 0.4G); PROTEIN 4G; CARB 24G; FIBER 1G; CHOL 0MG; IRON 1MG; SODIUM 112MG; CALC 5MG

Whole-Wheat Pizza Dough

Dissolve 1¼ teaspoons yeast and ¼ teaspoon sugar in ⅔ cup warm water in a small bowl; let stand 5 minutes. Stir in 1 tablespoon olive oil and 2 teaspoons honey. Weigh or lightly spoon 5.6 ounces all-purpose flour (about 1¼ cups) and 3.2 ounces whole-wheat flour (about ⅔ cup) into dry measuring cups; level with a knife. Combine flours and ½ teaspoon salt in the bowl of a stand mixer, stirring with a whisk. Gradually add yeast mixture, beating at low speed until smooth. Turn dough out onto a lightly floured surface; knead until smooth and elastic (about 3 minutes). Place dough in a large bowl coated with cooking spray; turning to coat top. Cover and let rise in a warm place (85°), free from drafts, 1 hour or until doubled in size. (Gently press two fingers into dough. If indentation remains, dough has risen enough.) Punch dough down, and shape into a ball.

SERVES 8

CALORIES 129; FAT 2.3G (SAT 0.3G); SODIUM 141MG

roasted vegetable and ricotta
PIZZA

◇◇◇

HANDS-ON TIME: 12 MIN. TOTAL TIME: 56 MIN.

◇◇◇

Fresh ricotta and colorful roasted zucchini, mushrooms, and peppers elevate this pizza from common-place to gourmet. No pizza stone? Use a 16-inch pizza pan with holes for a crispy pizza crust. Bake it on the bottom rack of the oven to ensure even more crispiness.

◇◇◇

½ recipe Pizza Dough (page 76) or ½ recipe Whole-Wheat Pizza Dough (page 76) or 1 pound refrigerated fresh pizza dough
2 cups sliced cremini mushrooms
1 cup (¼-inch-thick) slices zucchini
¼ teaspoon freshly ground black pepper
1 medium yellow bell pepper, sliced
1 medium red onion, cut into thick slices
1½ tablespoons plus 1 teaspoon olive oil, divided
1 tablespoon yellow cornmeal
⅓ cup tomato sauce
1 cup (4 ounces) shredded part-skim mozzarella cheese, divided
½ teaspoon crushed red pepper
⅓ cup Homemade Ricotta Cheese (page 132) or part-skim ricotta cheese
2 tablespoons small basil leaves

1. Position an oven rack in the lowest setting; place a pizza stone on rack. Preheat oven to 500°.

2. Remove dough from refrigerator. Let stand, covered, 30 minutes.

3. Combine mushrooms and next 4 ingredients (through onion) in a large bowl; drizzle with 1½ tablespoons oil. Toss. Arrange vegetables on a jelly-roll pan. Bake at 500° for 15 minutes.

4. Punch dough down. Sprinkle a lightly floured baking sheet with cornmeal; roll dough out to 15-inch circle on prepared baking sheet. Brush dough with 1 teaspoon oil. Spread sauce over dough, leaving a ½-inch border. Sprinkle ½ cup mozzarella over sauce; top with vegetables. Sprinkle ½ cup mozzarella and red pepper over zucchini mixture. Dollop with ricotta. Slide pizza onto preheated pizza stone. Bake at 500° for 11 minutes or until crust is golden. Sprinkle with basil.

◇◇◇

SERVES 6 (SERVING SIZE: 2 SLICES)
CALORIES 347; FAT 11.1G (SAT 3.7G, MONO 4.4G, POLY 2G); PROTEIN 15G; CARB 49G; FIBER 3G; CHOL 15MG; IRON 3G; SODIUM 655MG; CALC 193MG

VARIATIONS

Use Pesto (page 168) or the Spinach-Herb Pesto in the recipe on page 171 instead of tomato sauce.

Or, in lieu of sauce, substitute Caramelized Onion Marmalade (page 159) or grilled pear slices to add a touch of sweetness and a little bit of moisture.

Add on ¼ cup sliced olives for color and savory flavor, or steamed asparagus spears cut into ½-inch pieces for added texture.

spinach and mushroom
CALZONES

HANDS-ON TIME: 41 MIN. TOTAL TIME: 2 HR. 1 MIN.

2   teaspoons olive oil
¾   cup minced fresh onion (about 1 small)
2   garlic cloves, minced
1   (8-ounce) package presliced exotic
      mushroom blend (such as shiitake, cremini,
      and oyster)
1   (5-ounce) package fresh baby spinach,
      chopped
1¼   cups part-skim ricotta cheese
¼   cup shredded part-skim mozzarella cheese
2   tablespoons grated fresh pecorino Romano
      cheese
2   teaspoons chopped fresh basil
1   teaspoon chopped fresh oregano
½   teaspoon freshly ground black pepper
¼   teaspoon salt
⅛   teaspoon crushed red pepper
Cooking spray
1   recipe Whole-Wheat Pizza Dough (page 76)
1   tablespoon water
1   large egg

1. Heat a large nonstick skillet over medium-high heat. Add oil to pan; swirl to coat. Add onion and garlic; sauté 3 minutes or until tender and beginning to brown. Add mushrooms; sauté 4 minutes or until liquid mostly evaporates. Add spinach; sauté 2 minutes or until spinach wilts. Spoon mixture into a bowl; cool 5 minutes. Stir ricotta and next 7 ingredients (through crushed pepper) into spinach mixture.

2. Preheat oven to 450°.

3. Line a large baking sheet with foil. Coat foil with cooking spray. Divide dough into 8 equal portions. Roll each portion into a 6-inch circle on a lightly floured surface. Spoon about ¼ cup spinach mixture onto half of each circle, leaving a ½-inch border. Fold dough over filling; pinch edges of dough with fingers to seal.

4. Place calzones on prepared baking sheet. Make three small cuts on top. Combine 1 tablespoon water and egg, stirring with a whisk. Brush calzones with egg mixture.

5. Bake at 450° for 20 minutes or until browned. Transfer calzones to a wire rack. Cool completely. To freeze, place on a baking sheet in the freezer, and then transfer to a zip-top plastic freezer bag for up to 1 month. Thaw in the fridge, and warm in an oven or toaster oven.

SERVES 8 (SERVING SIZE: 1 CALZONE)
CALORIES 471; FAT 15.8G (SAT 6.1G, MONO 6.5G, POLY 1.4G); PROTEIN 22G; CARB 62G; FIBER 5G; CHOL 30MG; IRON 5MG; SODIUM 635MG; CALC 336MG

STEP 1   STEP 2

cheesy herb
BREADSTICKS

❖❖❖❖❖❖❖❖❖❖❖❖❖❖❖❖❖❖❖❖❖❖❖❖❖❖❖❖❖❖❖❖❖❖❖

HANDS-ON TIME: 29 MIN. TOTAL TIME: 1 HR. 13 MIN.

❖❖❖❖❖❖❖❖❖❖❖❖❖❖❖❖❖❖❖❖❖❖❖❖❖❖❖❖❖❖❖❖❖❖❖

These from-scratch breadsticks don't contain the saturated fat and excess sodium found in many store-bought varieties. Another plus: The kitchen will smell divine while they're baking. Serve them while they're still warm.

❖❖❖❖❖❖❖❖❖❖❖❖❖❖❖❖❖❖❖❖❖❖❖❖❖❖❖❖❖❖❖❖❖❖❖

<table>
<tr><td colspan="2">Cooking spray</td></tr>
<tr><td>½</td><td>recipe Pizza Dough (page 76)</td></tr>
<tr><td>2</td><td>tablespoons olive oil</td></tr>
<tr><td>2</td><td>ounces fresh Parmesan cheese, finely shredded</td></tr>
<tr><td>1</td><td>tablespoon chopped fresh oregano</td></tr>
<tr><td>½</td><td>teaspoon salt</td></tr>
<tr><td>¼</td><td>teaspoon freshly ground black pepper</td></tr>
</table>

1. Coat 2 baking sheets with cooking spray. Divide dough into 24 equal portions. Roll each piece into a 6-inch-long rope. Place 12 ropes on each prepared pan. Brush ropes with olive oil.
2. Preheat oven to 450°.
3. Combine cheese and oregano in a small bowl. Sprinkle breadsticks evenly with salt and pepper; sprinkle with cheese mixture. Cover and let dough rise in a warm place (85°), free from drafts, 20 minutes or until doubled in size.
4. Uncover breadsticks, and bake at 450° for 12 minutes or until golden brown. Remove breadsticks from pans. Cool completely on wire racks.

❖❖❖❖❖❖❖❖❖❖❖❖❖❖❖❖❖❖❖❖❖❖❖❖❖❖❖❖❖❖❖❖❖❖❖

SERVES 24 (SERVING SIZE: 1 BREADSTICK)
CALORIES 65; FAT 2.6G (SAT 0.7G, MONO 1.5G, POLY 0.3G); PROTEIN 2G; CARB 8G; FIBER 0G; CHOL 2MG; IRON 1MG; SODIUM 127MG; CALC 32MG

VARIATIONS

Substitute an Italian seasoning blend for the oregano.

Switch out the herbs for ½ teaspoon garlic powder, and sprinkle the breadsticks with poppy seeds and sesame seeds.

Substitute Asiago cheese for the Parmesan.

Serve with Slow-Cooker Marinara (page 257) on the side for dipping.

steamed
CURRIED CHICKEN BUNS

HANDS-ON TIME: 56 MIN. TOTAL TIME: 3 HR. 16 MIN.

◆◆◆◆ TECHNIQUE ◆◆◆◆

Shaping Steamed Buns

Pretty steamed buns (called *bao*) are not difficult to make, but they might take some practice to form. Here are some tips for sealing them properly:

STEP 1

1. After you have placed the filling in the middle of the dough circle, bring the edges of the dough over the filling, pushing the filling down as you form pleats in the dough. The dough will stretch as you pull it.

STEP 2

2. Grab the top of the pleats, and twist to seal the bao closed.

---

1   teaspoon Madras curry powder
1   pound skinless, boneless chicken breast
Cooking spray
1   cup thinly sliced green onions
½   teaspoon salt, divided
3   tablespoons hot mango chutney
1   tablespoon rice wine vinegar
1   tablespoon fresh lime juice
1   tablespoon low-sodium soy sauce
2   teaspoons honey
1   tablespoon minced peeled fresh ginger
2   large garlic cloves, minced
¼   cup chopped fresh cilantro
1   cup warm water (100° to 110°)
3   tablespoons sugar
1   package dry yeast (about 2¼ teaspoons)
14.6 ounces all-purpose flour (about 3¼ cups)
3   tablespoons canola oil
1½ teaspoons baking powder

1. Rub curry powder over chicken. Heat a grill pan over medium-high heat. Coat pan with cooking spray. Add chicken; cook 4 minutes on each side or until chicken is done. Remove chicken from pan, and let stand 10 minutes.
2. Cut chicken into thin strips. Place chicken in a bowl. Add onions, ¼ teaspoon salt, and next 8 ingredients (through cilantro); stir well to combine. Cover and refrigerate.
3. Combine 1 cup warm water, sugar, and yeast; let stand 5 minutes.

4. Weigh or lightly spoon flour into dry measuring cups; level with a knife. Add flour, oil, and ¼ teaspoon salt to yeast mixture; stir until a soft dough forms. Turn dough out onto a lightly floured surface. Knead until smooth and elastic (about 10 minutes). Place dough in a bowl coated with cooking spray, turning to coat top. Cover and let rise in a warm place (85°), free from drafts, 1½ hours or until doubled in size. (Gently press two fingers into dough. If indentation remains, dough has risen enough.)
5. Punch dough down; let rest 5 minutes. Turn dough out onto a clean surface; knead in baking powder. Let dough rest 5 minutes.
6. Divide dough into 15 equal portions, forming each into a ball. Working with 1 dough ball at a time (cover remaining dough balls to keep from drying), roll ball into a 5-inch circle. Place ¼ cup filling in center of dough circle. Bring up sides to cover filling and meet on top. Pinch and twist to seal. Repeat procedure.
7. Arrange 5 buns, seam sides down, 1 inch apart, in each tier of a 3-tiered bamboo steamer. Stack tiers; cover with lid. Add water to a large skillet to depth of 1 inch; bring to a boil over medium-high heat. Place steamer in boiling water in pan; steam 15 minutes or until buns are puffed and set. Cool 10 minutes.

SERVES 15 (SERVING SIZE: 1 BUN)

CALORIES 187; FAT 4.1G (SAT 0.5G, MONO 2.2G, POLY 1.1G); PROTEIN 10G; CARB 27G; FIBER 1G; CHOL 19MG; IRON 2MG; SODIUM 204MG; CALC 46MG

DAIRY-FREE

NUT-FREE

EGG-FREE

classic PASTA DOUGH

HANDS-ON TIME: 34 MIN. TOTAL TIME: 44 MIN.

Making basic pasta is a pleasure, and it's easier and more forgiving than you think. Look for Italian 00 flour at gourmet or online stores. This soft wheat flour gives the pasta a silkier texture.

5.6 ounces soft wheat flour (about 1¼ cups)
⅛ teaspoon fine sea salt
2 large eggs

1. Weigh or lightly spoon flour into dry measuring cups; level with a knife. Place flour, salt, and eggs in a food processor; pulse 10 times or until mixture is crumbly (dough will not form a ball). Turn dough out onto a lightly floured surface; knead until smooth and elastic (about 4 minutes). Shape dough into a disc; wrap with plastic wrap. Let dough stand at room temperature 20 minutes.

2. Unwrap dough. Divide dough into 8 equal portions. Working with 1 portion at a time (keep remaining dough covered to prevent drying), pass dough through pasta rollers of a pasta machine on the widest setting. Fold dough in half crosswise; fold in half again. Pass dough through rollers again. Move width gauge to next setting; pass pasta through rollers. Continue moving width gauge to narrower settings; pass dough through rollers once at each setting to form 8 (15 x 3–inch) pasta strips. Lay strips flat on a lightly floured surface; cover. Repeat procedure with remaining dough portions.

Note: If you don't plan to cook fresh pasta within a day, lay it out on trays. Lightly flour the pasta, and separate it so it doesn't stick together. Store it in the refrigerator for up to 2 days. To freeze, place the trays in the freezer, and freeze just until the pasta is set. Then, transfer to zip-top plastic bags. Don't defrost the pasta before you cook it; simply drop it into boiling water.

SERVES 4 (SERVING SIZE: 2 OUNCES UNCOOKED PASTA)
CALORIES 178; FAT 2.9G (SAT 0.8G, MONO 1G, POLY 0.3G); PROTEIN 7G; CARB 30G; FIBER 0G; CHOL 106MG; IRON 1MG; SODIUM 107MG; CALC 21MG

STEP 1

STEP 2

STEP 3

STEP 4

TECHNIQUE

Shaping Pasta

You can use the sheets made in the recipe as you would lasagna, or try these shapes:

1. To make makaruni, after the dough rests, simply divide the dough into 8 equal portions; divide each portion into 14 subportions. Roll each subportion between your palms to form plump, short strands. Toss each noodle onto a floured baking sheet, and roll in flour to prevent sticking.

2. To make tagliolini, fettuccine, or pappardelle, lay one pasta sheet flat, and dust it lightly with flour. Fold in the ends so they meet in the middle. (Make sure to sprinkle any dough surfaces that touch with flour to prevent sticking.) Then fold the sheet in the middle, like closing a book, and fold in half again. You'll have a narrow rectangle with eight layers of pasta.

3. Slice this rectangle crosswise into strips, which will unfold as long flat noodles. For tagliolini, cut the strips ¼ inch wide. For fettuccine, cut the strips ½ inch wide. For pappardelle, cut the strips 1½ inches wide.

4. Unfurl the layered noodles by shaking them open (unfold carefully if they're stuck). Sprinkle lightly with flour, and then toss them with a bit more flour so they don't stick together.

NUT-FREE

RAVIOLI
with herbed ricotta filling

HANDS-ON TIME: 26 MIN. TOTAL TIME: 61 MIN.

Fresh ravioli, made with your own pasta dough and homemade ricotta cheese, are molto buona. These are topped with a simple garlic sauce, or you can make just the ravioli and freeze.

Ravioli:

- ¾ cup (6 ounces) Homemade Ricotta Cheese (page 132) or whole-milk ricotta cheese
- ¼ cup (1 ounce) grated fresh Parmigiano-Reggiano cheese
- 2 tablespoons finely chopped fresh basil
- ½ teaspoon grated lemon rind
- ¼ teaspoon freshly ground black pepper
- 1 large egg
- 1 recipe Classic Pasta Dough (page 87)
- 6 quarts water
- 2 tablespoons fine sea salt

Sauce:

- 2 tablespoons extra-virgin olive oil
- 2 garlic cloves, minced
- ¼ cup chopped fresh basil
- 1 ounce shaved fresh Parmigiano-Reggiano cheese

1. To prepare ravioli, place ricotta in a cheesecloth-lined colander; drain 30 minutes. Combine ricotta, grated Parmigiano-Reggiano, and next 4 ingredients (through egg), stirring until well combined.
2. Place 1 (15 x 3–inch) Classic Pasta Dough sheet on a lightly floured surface. Spoon 1½ teaspoons filling mixture 1½ inches from left edge in the center of sheet. Spoon 1½ teaspoons filling mixture at 3-inch intervals along the length of sheet. Moisten edges and in between each filling portion with water; place 1 (15 x 3–inch) pasta sheet on top, pressing to seal. Cut pasta sheet crosswise into 5 (3 x 3–inch) ravioli, trimming edges with a sharp knife or pastry wheel. Place ravioli on a lightly floured baking sheet (cover with a damp towel to prevent drying). Repeat procedure with remaining pasta sheets and filling mixture to form 20 ravioli.
3. Bring 6 quarts water and salt to a boil in an 8-quart pot. Add half of ravioli to pot; cook 1½ minutes or until no longer translucent. Remove ravioli from water with a slotted spoon. Repeat procedure with remaining ravioli.
4. To prepare sauce, heat a small skillet over low heat. Add oil to pan; swirl to coat. Add garlic to pan; cook 6 minutes or until garlic is tender. Remove from heat. Place 5 ravioli in each of 4 shallow bowls; drizzle each serving with 1½ teaspoons garlic oil. Top each serving with 1 tablespoon basil and ¼ of shaved Parmigiano-Reggiano. Serve immediately.

SERVES 4

CALORIES 379; FAT 18.6G (SAT 7.1G, MONO 8.1G, POLY 1.9G); PROTEIN 22G; CARB 32G; FIBER 4G; CHOL 164MG; IRON 1MG; SODIUM 665MG; CALC 419MG

homemade GNOCCHI

HANDS-ON TIME: 35 MIN. TOTAL TIME: 1 HR. 46 MIN.

Make these plump pillows of pasta ahead, and freeze them for a quick weekday meal. Or try them with arugula in a Lemon-Thyme Butter Sauce (page 93). You don't need any special gadgets to make these melt-in-the-mouth treats—just your hands and a fork.

MORE IDEAS

Need a sauce to finish the dish? No matter which you choose, gnocchi tastes better if it cooks in the sauce for just a minute. Try one of these:

• Browned butter and sage. Melt 3 tablespoons of butter in a saucepan until it foams and subsides. Spoon in a few tablespoons of cooking water from the gnocchi, and stir to thicken the sauce. Add fresh sage leaves.

• Béchamel Sauce (page 249)

• Slow-Cooker Marinara (page 257) with a sprinkle of Parmesan cheese

• Pesto (page 168)

2   (12-ounce) baking potatoes, unpeeled
¾   teaspoon kosher salt
4.5 ounces all-purpose flour (about 1 cup)
2   tablespoons chopped fresh chives
¼   teaspoon freshly ground black pepper
2   large eggs, lightly beaten
6   quarts boiling water

1. Place potatoes in a saucepan; cover with water. Bring to a boil over medium-high heat. Cook 40 minutes; drain. Cool; peel. Press potato flesh through a ricer. Spread potatoes on a baking sheet; sprinkle with salt. Cool.

2. Scoop potatoes into a large bowl. Weigh or lightly spoon flour into a dry measuring cup. Add flour to potatoes, and toss. Form a well in center. Add chives, pepper, and eggs; stir. Turn dough out onto a lightly floured surface. Gently knead just until dough comes together (about 1 minute).

3. Cut dough into 4 equal portions, and roll each into a 22-inch-long rope. Cut each rope into 22 pieces. Score gnocchi with a fork. Cook half of gnocchi 3 minutes in boiling water. Repeat with remaining gnocchi; drain.

Note: You can freeze gnocchi for up to 3 months. To freeze, place them spaced apart on a parchment-lined baking sheet. Freeze until frozen solid, at least 1 hour, so they won't stick together when stored. Transfer to a zip-top bag. To cook, toss half the frozen gnocchi in boiling water for about 5 minutes. Repeat with remaining gnocchi.

SERVES 4 (SERVING SIZE: ABOUT 22 GNOCCHI)

CALORIES 287; FAT 2.8G (SAT 0.9G, MONO 1G, POLY 0.7G); PROTEIN 10G; CARB 55G; FIBER 3G; CHOL 93MG; IRON 3MG; SODIUM 405MG; CALC 43MG

GNOCCHI AND ARUGULA
with lemon-thyme butter sauce

HANDS-ON TIME: 37 MIN. TOTAL TIME: 1 HR. 57 MIN.

Success with a simple recipe comes down to classic ingredients: shallots, dry white wine, butter, lemon, and thyme. Make this elegant gnocchi as a side for roasted chicken, or serve it as a main dish with vegetables on the side (or stirred in) to round out your meal.

1 lemon
Cooking spray
$1/3$ cup finely chopped shallots
$1/2$ cup fat-free, lower-sodium chicken broth
$1/4$ cup dry white wine
2 tablespoons butter
2 teaspoons chopped fresh thyme leaves
4 cups fresh arugula
1 recipe Homemade Gnocchi (page 90)
$1/4$ cup (1 ounce) shaved fresh pecorino Romano cheese

1. Grate rind and squeeze juice from lemon to measure $1/2$ teaspoon and 2 tablespoons, respectively.
2. Heat a large skillet over medium-high heat. Coat pan with cooking spray. Add shallots to pan; sauté 2 minutes. Stir in chicken broth, wine, and lemon juice. Bring to boil; cook, uncovered, 4 minutes or until reduced to $1/2$ cup. Remove from heat; stir in butter, thyme, and lemon rind. Transfer sauce to a bowl, and keep warm.
3. Wipe skillet with paper towels. Coat pan with cooking spray. Place pan over medium-high heat. Immediately add arugula, and cook, tossing constantly with tongs, 1 minute or until arugula wilts. Reduce heat to medium-low; add cooked gnocchi and lemon sauce, stirring to coat.
4. Place gnocchi mixture into each of 5 shallow bowls; sprinkle evenly with cheese.

SERVES 5 (SERVING SIZE: 1 CUP GNOCCHI MIXTURE AND ABOUT 1 TABLESPOON CHEESE)

CALORIES 318; FAT 9.7G (SAT 4.8G, MONO 2.3G, POLY 0.8G); PROTEIN 10G; CARB 46G; FIBER 3G; CHOL 92MG; IRON 2MG; SODIUM 528MG; CALC 101MG

whole-wheat

HAMBURGER BUNS

HANDS-ON TIME: 15 MIN. TOTAL TIME: 2 HR. 35 MIN.

Keep these homemade buns on hand to make burgers you'll be proud to serve. A mix of whole-wheat and white flour keeps the buns light, milk makes them soft, and honey adds a slight sweetness.

MORE IDEAS

To make slider buns, about 3 inches in diameter, divide the dough into 24 portions, and bake for 12 to 15 minutes or until they're golden. Use the full-size or slider buns for burgers or sandwiches of all types.

1   cup water
½   cup 1% low-fat milk
2   tablespoons canola oil
1   tablespoon honey
7.13 ounces whole-wheat flour (about 1½ cups)
11.25 ounces all-purpose flour (about 2½ cups), divided
1   teaspoon kosher salt
1   package dry yeast (about 2¼ teaspoons)
Cooking spray
1   large egg, lightly beaten

1. Combine first 4 ingredients in a medium saucepan. Cook over low heat until a thermometer registers 120° to 130°.

2. Weigh or lightly spoon whole-wheat flour and 6.75 ounces all-purpose flour (about 1½ cups) into dry measuring cups; level with a knife. Combine flours, salt, and yeast in the bowl of a stand mixer with dough hook attached. Add very warm water mixture; beat at medium-high speed 2 minutes or until blended. Add 1 cup all-purpose flour, ¼ cup at a time, beating until dough pulls away from the side of the bowl and is no longer sticky. (Dough will be slightly tacky, but not sticky.) Knead with mixer until smooth and elastic, about 5 minutes.

3. Place dough in a large bowl coated with cooking spray. Cover and let rise in a warm place (85°), free from drafts, 30 minutes or until doubled in size. (Gently press two fingers into dough. If indentation remains, dough has risen enough.)

4. Punch dough down; divide into 12 equal portions. Shape portions into smooth balls. Place on parchment paper–lined baking sheets, pressing to flatten slightly. Coat with cooking spray. Cover and let rise 30 minutes or until doubled in size.

5. Preheat oven to 400°.

6. Brush buns with beaten egg. Bake at 400° for 18 to 20 minutes or until lightly browned. Remove from oven; cover loosely with foil. Cool 15 minutes. Uncover and cool completely.

Note: If not using within 1 day, place the buns in a large heavy-duty zip-top plastic bag. Seal bag, removing as much air as possible, and freeze for up to 1 month.

SERVES 12 (SERVING SIZE: 1 BUN)
CALORIES 194; FAT 3.7G (SAT 0.6G, MONO 1.9G, POLY 1.2G); PROTEIN 6G; CARB 35G; FIBER 3G; CHOL 16MG; IRON 2MG; SODIUM 172MG; CALC 25MG

Thai turkey
BURGERS

HANDS-ON TIME: 28 MIN. TOTAL TIME: 28 MIN.

Turkey burgers can often taste like cardboard, but these are juicy and bursting with flavor. The key is to use ground turkey (not ground turkey breast), which includes white meat and richer and more flavorful dark meat. The radish salad and the topping of fresh basil leaves instead of lettuce add even more zing.

VARIATIONS

For classic flavor, stir in finely diced onion, fresh chopped parsley, and minced garlic.

For a Southwestern take, spice the meat with a finely chopped chipotle chile in adobo sauce, minced onion, salt, and chopped fresh cilantro.

Go for a kebab flavor by working garam masala, fresh ginger, minced garlic, and plain yogurt into the meat.

For an easy Asian-inspired take, add minced water chestnuts for crunch, and toss in lots of chopped green onions and a little soy sauce.

1   pound ground turkey
¼   cup chopped fresh cilantro
2   tablespoons lower-sodium soy sauce
1   tablespoon minced fresh ginger
1   tablespoon lemongrass paste
1   tablespoon dark sesame oil
½   teaspoon grated lime rind
¼   teaspoon ground red pepper
3   garlic cloves, minced
½   cup shredded radishes (about 6 medium)
½   cup shredded carrot
½   cup shredded seeded English cucumber
1   tablespoon fresh lime juice
¼   teaspoon dark sesame oil
¼   teaspoon freshly ground black pepper
Cooking spray
4   Whole-Wheat Hamburger Buns (page 94), halved
¾   cup basil leaves

1. Combine first 9 ingredients in a medium bowl, mixing gently. Let stand 5 minutes.
2. Divide turkey mixture into 4 equal portions, shaping each into a ½-inch-thick patty. Press thumb in center of each patty, leaving a nickel-sized indentation.
3. Combine radishes and next 5 ingredients (through black pepper), stirring gently; let stand while patties cook.
4. Preheat grill to high heat.
5. Coat grill rack with cooking spray; place on grill. Coat patties with cooking spray. Grill patties 3 minutes. Carefully turn patties over, and grill 3 minutes or until done. During last 2 minutes of cooking patties, coat cut sides of buns with cooking spray; place, cut sides down, on grill rack. Grill 1 minute or until golden.
6. Place patties on bottom halves of buns. Spoon about ⅓ cup radish mixture on top of each patty, using a slotted spoon. Top evenly with basil, and cover with bun tops.

SERVES 4 (SERVING SIZE: 1 BURGER)

CALORIES 406; FAT 15.1G (SAT 3.3G, MONO 5.7G, POLY 5.9G); PROTEIN 29G; CARB 40G; FIBER 4G; CHOL 81MG; IRON 4MG; SODIUM 548MG; CALC 58MG

honey
WHOLE-WHEAT BREAD

HANDS-ON TIME: 24 MIN. TOTAL TIME: 4 HR. 9 MIN.

Strange things appear in the ingredients list of store-bought bread, including sugarcane fiber, dough conditioners, and distilled monoglycerides. Make your own from simple ingredients instead.

2   packages dry yeast (4½ teaspoons)
½   cup honey, divided
3   cups warm water (100° to 110°)
22.6 ounces bread flour (about 4¾ cups)
16.6 ounces whole-wheat flour (about 3½ cups)
3   tablespoons butter, melted
2   teaspoons salt
Cooking spray

1. Dissolve yeast and ¼ cup honey in warm water in bowl of a stand mixer; let stand 5 minutes.
2. Weigh or lightly spoon flours into dry measuring cups; level with a knife. Stir 19 ounces (about 4 cups) bread flour into yeast mixture. Add butter, salt, and ¼ cup honey; beat 1 minute. Add whole-wheat flour, 1 cup at a time, until a soft dough forms. Turn dough out onto a lightly floured surface. Knead until smooth and elastic (about 4 minutes); add enough of remaining bread flour, ¼ cup at a time, to prevent dough from sticking to hands (dough will feel slightly sticky).
3. Place dough in a large bowl coated with cooking spray, turning to coat top. Cover and let rise in a warm place (85°), free from drafts, 1 hour or until doubled in size. (Gently press two fingers into dough. If indentation remains, dough has risen enough.) Punch dough down; cover and let rest 15 minutes. Divide dough into thirds. Working with 1 portion of dough at a time (cover remaining dough to prevent drying), roll portion into a 14 x 7–inch rectangle on a lightly floured surface. Roll up rectangle tightly, starting with a short edge, pressing firmly to eliminate air pockets; pinch seam and ends to seal. Place roll, seam side down, in an 8 x 4–inch loaf pan coated with cooking spray. Repeat with remaining 2 portions of dough. Cover and let rise 40 minutes or until dough rises 1-inch higher than tops of pans.
4. Preheat oven to 350°.
5. Bake loaves at 350° for 30 minutes or until loaves are lightly browned and sound hollow when tapped. Remove from pans; cool completely on wire racks.

Note: This recipe yields 3 loaves that freeze nicely. Once the bread has cooled, cut each loaf into 14 slices. Place each loaf in a zip-top plastic bag, remove as much air as possible, and store in the freezer for up to 3 months.

SERVES 42 (SERVING SIZE: 1 SLICE)
CALORIES 115; FAT 1.5G (SAT 0.6G, MONO 0.4G, POLY 0.3G); PROTEIN 3G; CARB 23G; FIBER 2G; CHOL 2MG; IRON 1MG; SODIUM 121MG; CALC 7MG

turkey-apple-Gouda MELT

HANDS-ON TIME: 10 MIN. TOTAL TIME: 10 MIN.

Tart Granny Smith apple slices, peppery arugula, and honey mustard perk up the flavors of a turkey and cheese sandwich and add some fiber, too. If you don't own a panini grill, use a large nonstick skillet and flip the sandwiches, cooking until they are browned on each side and the cheese is melted.

8   teaspoons Honey Mustard (page 173)
8   slices Honey Whole-Wheat Bread (page 99)
6   ounces thinly sliced lower-sodium
    oven-roasted turkey breast
½   Granny Smith apple, thinly sliced
3   ounces Gouda cheese, shredded
½   cup arugula leaves
Cooking spray

1. Preheat panini grill.
2. Spread 1 teaspoon Honey Mustard evenly over each bread slice. Top each of 4 bread slices evenly with turkey, apple, cheese, and arugula. Top sandwiches with remaining bread slices. Coat outsides of sandwiches with cooking spray. Place sandwiches on panini grill; cook 3 minutes or until golden and cheese is melted. Cut panini in half before serving.

SERVES 4 (SERVING SIZE: 1 SANDWICH)
CALORIES 383; FAT 10.4G (SAT 5.2G, MONO 3.3G, POLY 1G); PROTEIN 23G; CARB 54G; FIBER 4G; CHOL 47MG; IRON 3MG; SODIUM 790MG; CALC 185MG

MORE IDEAS

Use this recipe as a base for a wide variety of flavor combinations: Try romaine lettuce and Four-Herb Green Goddess Dressing (page 183) or Homemade Ricotta Cheese (page 132), roasted red peppers, and fresh arugula. For a classic caprese, layer on Homemade Mozzarella (page 120) and tomato slices with fresh basil leaves.

fig and onion
FOCACCIA

HANDS-ON TIME: 15 MIN. TOTAL TIME: 40 MIN.

There's something heavenly about the combination of blue cheese, sautéed onions, and sticky sweet figs on bread. Typically focaccia is baked in a sheet pan and rises a little higher than regular pizza crust. These squares serve a crowd.

VARIATIONS

If you'd like to prepare a classic focaccia, you'll just need to brush on some olive oil and sprinkle the dough with salt and fresh herbs.

Or, top the dough with a light layer of Slow-Cooker Marinara (page 257) and Parmesan or Romano cheese.

½   cup chopped dried Black Mission figs
1½ tablespoons olive oil, divided
1½ cups vertically sliced onion
2   tablespoons balsamic vinegar
½   recipe Pizza Dough (page 76)
Cooking spray
½   cup crumbled blue cheese
½   teaspoon chopped fresh rosemary
¼   teaspoon freshly ground black pepper

1. Preheat oven to 425°.
2. Place figs and boiling water to cover in a bowl. Cover and let stand 5 minutes. Drain.
3. Heat a medium nonstick skillet over medium heat. Add 1½ teaspoons oil to pan; swirl to coat. Add onion; sauté 8 minutes or until onion is tender and golden. Add vinegar; cook, uncovered, 2 minutes or until liquid evaporates.
4. Press dough into a 12 x 10–inch rectangle on a large baking sheet coated with cooking spray. Make indentations in top of dough using the handle of a wooden spoon or your fingertips. Gently brush dough with 1 tablespoon olive oil. Sprinkle dough with onion and figs. Sprinkle with cheese, rosemary, and pepper.
5. Bake at 425° for 20 minutes or until lightly browned. Cut into rectangles.

SERVES 12 (SERVING SIZE: 1 PIECE)
CALORIES 148; FAT 5G (SAT 1.5G, MONO 2.6G, POLY 0.5G); PROTEIN 4G; CARB 22G; FIBER 1G; CHOL 4MG; IRON 1MG; SODIUM 155MG; CALC 47MG

whole-wheat
PITA BREAD

HANDS-ON TIME: 25 MIN. TOTAL TIME: 1 HR. 51 MIN.

Flatbreads exist in just about every culture in the world. Homebaked, from-scratch pitas have a far superior texture than the store-bought variety in a plastic bag. You can also bake these pitas on a pizza stone.

1 **cup plus 2 tablespoons warm water (100° to 110°)**
1 **tablespoon honey**
1 **package dry yeast (about 2¼ teaspoons)**
13.1 **ounces bread flour (about 2¾ cups), divided**
2.4 **ounces whole-wheat flour (about ½ cup)**
2 **tablespoons olive oil**
¾ **teaspoon salt**
Cooking spray

1. Combine first 3 ingredients in a large bowl, stirring to dissolve yeast; let stand 5 minutes. Weigh or lightly spoon 11.9 ounces bread flour (about 2½ cups) and whole-wheat flour into dry measuring cups; level with a knife. Add flours, oil, and salt to yeast mixture; beat with a mixer at medium speed until smooth. Turn dough out onto a floured surface. Knead dough until smooth and elastic (about 10 minutes), adding enough of ¼ cup bread flour, 1 tablespoon at a time, to prevent dough from sticking to hands (dough will feel sticky).
2. Place dough in a large bowl coated with cooking spray, turning to coat top. Cover and let rise in a warm place (85°), free from drafts, 1 hour or until doubled in size. Punch dough down; cover and let rest 5 minutes.
3. Position oven rack on the lowest shelf. Preheat oven to 500°.
4. Roll dough into an 8-inch log. Divide dough into 8 equal portions. Working with 1 portion at a time, gently roll dough into a (6-inch) circle. Place 4 dough circles on each of 2 baking sheets coated with cooking spray. Let dough rest, uncovered, 15 minutes.
5. Bake, 1 sheet at a time, at 500° for 6 minutes or until puffed and bottom is browned. Transfer to middle oven rack; bake an additional 1 to 2 minutes or until golden. Cool on a wire rack.

Note: This recipe yields 8 pitas. To freeze, wrap the pitas in foil, and seal in a zip-top plastic bag. Thaw, and reheat in the foil in the oven when ready to use.

SERVES 16 (SERVING SIZE: 1 PITA HALF)
CALORIES 120; FAT 2.4G (SAT 0.3G, MONO 1.4G, POLY 0.4G); PROTEIN 4G; CARB 21G; FIBER 1G; CHOL 0MG; IRON 1MG; SODIUM 112MG; CALC 5MG

MORE IDEAS

In addition to making sandwiches, you can make your own pita chips. See page 192 for details. Then serve them with an assortment of dips, such as any of the hummus recipes on page 229 or Tzatziki on page 116.

chicken-tzatziki
PITA

HANDS-ON TIME: 15 MIN. TOTAL TIME: 15 MIN.

Go Greek with this pita sandwich stuffed with salad. The homemade Tzatziki also makes a great dip with your pita bread as a snack or appetizer.

MORE IDEAS

• Serve them with any kind of hummus (page 229)—all are tasty.

• Stuff the pitas with fresh tomatoes, chopped romaine, cucumbers, kalamata olives, and feta cheese.

• Make a caprese sandwich with Homemade Mozzarella slices (page 120), fresh tomatoes, fresh basil, and a drizzle of olive oil.

• Pita halves hold salad items better than sliced bread, so experiment with fillings like Caprese "Salsa" Zucchini with Sea Salt (page 122).

¼   cup Tzatziki (page 116)
2   Whole-Wheat Pita Breads (page 105), cut in half
8   (¼-inch-thick) slices plum tomato
4   (⅛-inch-thick) slices small red onion
1⅓   cups thinly sliced cooked chicken breast
1   cup mixed salad greens

1. Spread 1 tablespoon Tzatziki inside each pita half. Place 2 tomato slices and 1 onion slice in each pita half. Stuff each half with ⅓ cup chicken and ¼ cup salad greens.

SERVES 4 (SERVING SIZE: 1 PITA HALF)
CALORIES 241; FAT 6.9G (SAT 1.5G, MONO 3.6G, POLY 1G); PROTEIN 21G; CARB 24G; FIBER 2G; CHOL 41MG; IRON 2MG; SODIUM 236MG; CALC 40MG

corn
TORTILLAS

✦✦✦✦✦✦✦✦✦✦✦✦✦✦✦✦✦✦✦✦✦✦✦✦✦✦✦✦✦✦✦✦✦✦✦

HANDS-ON TIME: 50 MIN. TOTAL TIME: 65 MIN.

✦✦✦✦✦✦✦✦✦✦✦✦✦✦✦✦✦✦✦✦✦✦✦✦✦✦✦✦✦✦✦✦✦✦✦

15.75 ounces instant masa harina (about 3½ cups)

2⅓ cups water

½ teaspoon salt

1. Weigh or lightly spoon masa harina into dry measuring cups; level with a knife. Combine masa harina, 2⅓ cups water, and salt in a bowl, stirring until a soft dough forms. Knead 30 seconds or until smooth. Cover and let stand 15 minutes.

2. Divide dough into 16 equal portions, and shape each portion into a ball. Working with 1 dough ball at a time, place ball between 2 sheets of heavy-duty plastic wrap (cover remaining balls to prevent drying). Place ball, still covered, in center of a tortilla press. Close press to flatten dough, moving handle from side to side. Rotate tortilla one-half turn. Press again. Remove dough. Carefully remove plastic wrap from flattened dough. Place between 2 sheets of wax paper. Repeat procedure with remaining dough balls.

3. Heat a 12-inch nonstick skillet over medium-high heat. Place 2 tortillas in pan; cook 1 to 2 minutes or until they begin to brown. Carefully turn tortillas over; cook 1 minute. Turn tortillas over once more, and cook 15 seconds. Repeat procedure with remaining tortillas.

Note: Transfer tortillas into a plastic bag. Store at room temperature for up to 1 week.

✦✦✦✦✦✦✦✦✦✦✦✦✦✦✦✦✦✦✦✦✦✦✦✦✦

SERVES 16 (SERVING SIZE: 1 TORTILLA)
CALORIES 96; FAT 1G (SAT 0.2G, MONO 0.3G, POLY 0.5G); PROTEIN 3G; CARB 20G; FIBER 2G; CHOL 0MG; IRON 2MG; SODIUM 73MG; CALC 39MG

Flour Tortillas

Weigh or lightly spoon 18 ounces all-purpose flour (about 4 cups) into dry measuring cups; level with a knife. Combine flour, 2 teaspoons baking powder, and 2 teaspoons salt in a bowl. Cut in 6 tablespoons vegan shortening (such as Earth Balance) with a pastry blender or 2 knives until mixture resembles coarse meal; make a well in center of mixture. Combine 1½ cups hot water and 1 tablespoon nonfat dry milk, and add to flour mixture. Stir until blended. Cover and let rest 20 minutes. Divide dough into 18 equal portions, shaping each portion into a ball (cover remaining dough to prevent drying). Roll out each ball into a 7-inch round. Heat a cast-iron skillet over medium-high heat. Cook each round 1 minute on each side or until lightly browned. Transfer tortillas into a plastic bag while still warm. Sealing the bag will keep the tortillas soft and flexible. Store at room temperature for up to 1 week.

✦✦✦✦✦✦✦✦✦✦✦✦✦✦✦✦✦✦✦✦✦✦✦✦✦

SERVES 18 (SERVING SIZE: 1 TORTILLA)
CALORIES 126; FAT 4G (SAT 1G); SODIUM 306MG

SMOKED CHICKEN TACOS
with spicy ranchero sauce and cilantro slaw

HANDS-ON TIME: 23 MIN. TOTAL TIME: 23 MIN.

Shredded smoked chicken spiced with chipotle and lime, a fresh slaw, and a zippy sauce keep this flavorful taco moist. Reheat premade tortillas in a cast-iron skillet on medium-high heat for up to 1 minute on each side.

³⁄₄ cup canned enchilada sauce
½ cup prechopped onion
½ chipotle chile, canned in adobo sauce
½ cup chopped fresh cilantro, divided
3 tablespoons fresh lime juice, divided
3 cups packaged angel hair slaw, coarsely chopped
1 cup shredded radishes (9 radishes)
¼ cup reduced-fat sour cream
¼ teaspoon salt
¼ teaspoon ground cumin
½ cup chopped poblano chile (about 1 small)
2 large garlic cloves, finely chopped
Cooking spray
2 cups shredded smoked chicken
1½ cups frozen fire-roasted whole-kernel corn, thawed
16 Corn Tortillas (page 108) or 6-inch corn tortillas, warmed
Lime wedges (optional)

1. Place enchilada sauce, onion, chipotle chile, ¼ cup cilantro, and 1 tablespoon lime juice in a blender or food processor; process until smooth.

2. Combine slaw, radishes, sour cream, ¼ cup cilantro, 2 tablespoons lime juice, salt, and cumin in a medium bowl, tossing well.

3. Heat a medium nonstick skillet over medium-high heat. Add poblano chile and garlic; coat vegetables with cooking spray. Sauté 4 minutes or until tender. Add chicken and corn; sauté 3 minutes or until thoroughly heated.

4. Place ¼ cup chicken mixture in center of each tortilla. Top with about 3 tablespoons slaw mixture and 1 tablespoon sauce. Fold tortillas in half; serve with lime wedges, if desired. Serve immediately.

SERVES 8 (SERVING SIZE: 2 TACOS)
CALORIES 355; FAT 7G (SAT 1.5G, MONO 2.7G, POLY 2G); PROTEIN 19G; CARB 56G; FIBER 6G; CHOL 33MG; IRON 5MG; SODIUM 468MG; CALC 115MG

VARIATIONS

Use shredded pork in this recipe as another option. If you can't find smoked chicken, shredded rotisserie chicken will work too, but the taste will be milder.

BBQ CHICKEN SOFT TACOS
with pineapple slaw

HANDS-ON TIME: 1 HR. 6 MIN. TOTAL TIME: 1 HR. 26 MIN.

These Southern-inspired soft tacos use barbecue sauce and coleslaw with the chicken, but add pineapple and feta for a sweet and salty burst. Rotisserie chicken and packaged coleslaw shave off some time for a doable weeknight meal.

2   cups packaged cabbage-and-carrot coleslaw
$1/3$ cup thinly sliced red onion
$1/3$ cup thinly sliced radishes
$1/3$ cup chopped fresh cilantro
$1/4$ cup chopped fresh pineapple
$2^1/2$ tablespoons reduced-fat sour cream
$2^1/2$ tablespoons canola mayonnaise
$2^1/4$ teaspoons fresh lime juice
2   cups shredded skinless, boneless rotisserie chicken breast
$1/3$ cup spicy barbecue sauce
8   Flour Tortillas (page 108), warmed
$1/4$ cup crumbled feta
Cilantro leaves (optional)

1. Combine first 5 ingredients in a large bowl. Combine sour cream, mayonnaise, and lime juice in a small bowl. Drizzle dressing over coleslaw mixture. Toss well.
2. Combine chicken and barbecue sauce. Place about $1/4$ cup chicken mixture on each tortilla. Top each with $1/3$ cup coleslaw mixture, and sprinkle with $1^1/2$ teaspoons feta cheese. Garnish with cilantro leaves, if desired.

SERVES 4 (SERVING SIZE: 2 SOFT TACOS)

CALORIES 281; FAT 10.9G (SAT 2.9G, MONO 4.2G, POLY 2.5G); PROTEIN 15G; CARB 29G; FIBER 1G; CHOL 37MG; IRON 2MG; SODIUM 562MG; CALC 98MG

VARIATIONS

The creamy slaw works with a variety of base ingredients. Use pulled pork, simply baked white fish (such as mahi mahi or tilapia), or baked tofu instead of the rotisserie chicken.

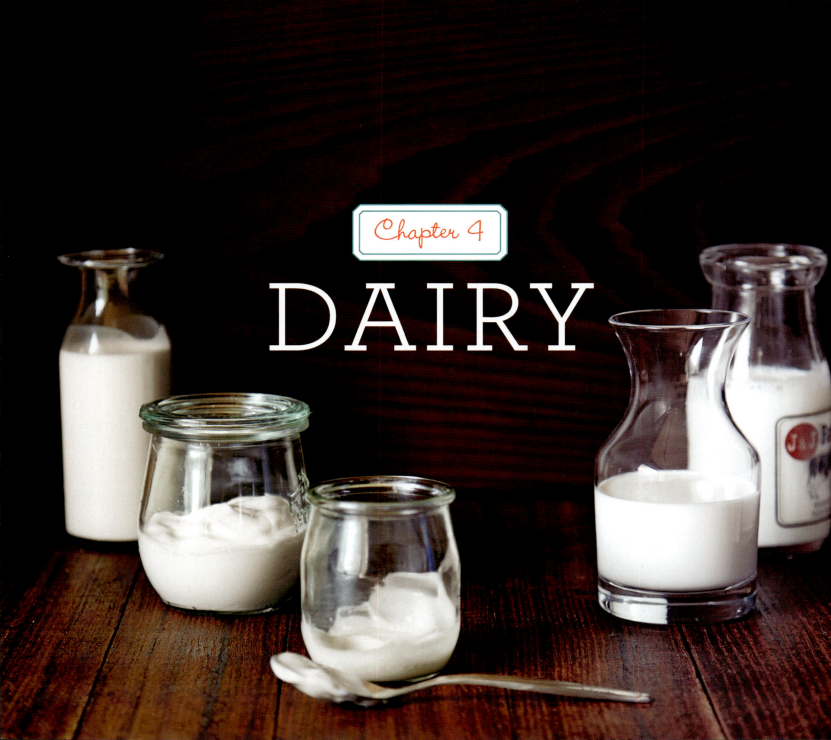

Chapter 4

DAIRY

Dairy products are often the items we most regularly buy at the grocery store—packaged yogurt, fresh cheese, ice cream. But many of these products can be easily prepared at home, allowing you to save money and avoid fillers and preservatives.

There may be an intimidation factor that keeps you from wanting to make these from scratch. But, you'll see from the recipes that you shouldn't feel overwhelmed. If you've got a thermometer, some cheese-cloth, and an ice-cream maker, you can prepare every recipe in this chapter.

Plus, we know you're busy, so there are smart shortcuts, like making mozzarella from curds instead of starting with milk. It's fast and easy. And speaking of fast, making fresh ricotta or mozzarella takes about a half hour. Once they cool you can eat them right away or store them in your refrigerator for later.

So, branch out. Try these homemade dairy products and the recipes that follow for fresh salads and dips, Ricotta Torte with Fresh Berry Topping (page 135), pizza, and Blackened Shrimp Tacos (page 131), to name just a few.

homemade
YOGURT

HANDS-ON TIME: 7 MIN. TOTAL TIME: 10 HR. 7 MIN.

Making yogurt from scratch really is easy. Be sure to save 2 tablespoons of your home-made yogurt so you'll have a starter for your next batch.

4 cups 1% low-fat milk

2 tablespoons plain low-fat yogurt

1. Place milk in a large saucepan; heat over medium-high heat until bubbles appear. Remove pan from heat. Let milk cool until it registers 110° to 112° on a thermometer.
2. Transfer milk to a large glass container. Stir yogurt into milk. Cover container tightly with plastic wrap. Place container in an unheated gas oven with the pilot light on, or an electric oven with the light left on for 8 hours or overnight. To check if yogurt is set, remove plastic wrap, and gently shake container to see if yogurt is very thick. If not, let it sit for a few hours longer. If it is thick, place container in refrigerator to chill.

Note: Store in refrigerator for up to 2 weeks.

SERVES 8 (SERVING SIZE: ½ CUP)
CALORIES 53; FAT 1.4G (SAT 0.8G, MONO 0.4G, POLY 0.1G); PROTEIN 4.2G; CARB 6.1G; FIBER 0G; CHOL 5MG; IRON 0.1MG; SODIUM 64MG; CALC 157MG

TZATZIKI

HANDS-ON TIME: 5 MIN. TOTAL TIME: 5 MIN.

After you've made this fresh Greek dip once, you won't need a recipe again. It's a simple mixture of yogurt, cucumber, lemon juice, and garlic, and you can play with the ratios to suit your tastes. Scoop it up with Whole-Wheat Pita Bread (page 105), serve with grilled meats or as a sauce for fish, dip falafel in it, or spoon it on wraps.

½ cup peeled, seeded, and shredded cucumber

½ cup Homemade Yogurt

1 tablespoon fresh lemon juice

¼ teaspoon salt

1 garlic clove, minced

1. Combine all ingredients in a medium bowl, stirring well.

Note: Store in an airtight container in refrigerator for up to 2 weeks.

SERVES 4 (SERVING SIZE: ABOUT ¼ CUP)
CALORIES 17; FAT 0.4G (SAT 0.2G, MONO 0.1G, POLY 0G); PROTEIN 1G; CARB 2G; FIBER 0G; CHOL 2MG; IRON 0MG; SODIUM 160MG; CALC 44MG

GRANOLA
with honeyed yogurt and baked figs

HANDS-ON TIME: 18 MIN. TOTAL TIME: 68 MIN.

This is no ordinary granola parfait. Ripe figs are coated in honey and vanilla, sprinkled with cinnamon, and baked until yielding. As an option, use Nutty Whole-Grain Granola (page 52) or Sunflower Granola (page 57) instead.

1   cup old-fashioned rolled oats
1/3   cup chopped pecans
1   large egg white
1 1/8   teaspoons vanilla extract, divided
2   tablespoons packed brown sugar
3/8   teaspoon ground cinnamon, divided
1/4   teaspoon salt, divided
1/8   teaspoon ground nutmeg
2   tablespoons maple syrup
Cooking spray
2   tablespoons plus 2 teaspoons honey, divided
9   firm, fresh dark-skinned figs, stemmed and quartered
3   cups Homemade Yogurt (page 116)

1. Preheat oven to 300°.
2. Combine oats and pecans in a small bowl. Combine egg white and 1/8 teaspoon vanilla in a medium bowl; beat egg mixture with a mixer at medium speed until foamy. Fold oat mixture into egg white mixture. Combine brown sugar, 1/4 teaspoon cinnamon, 1/8 teaspoon salt, and nutmeg; fold sugar mixture into oat mixture. Fold in maple syrup.
3. Spread granola evenly on a foil-lined baking sheet coated with cooking spray. Bake at 300° for 25 minutes, stirring once. Remove from oven; stir to loosen granola from foil. Cool on a wire rack.
4. Increase oven temperature to 350°.
5. Combine 2 teaspoons honey and 1 teaspoon vanilla in a large bowl; add figs, stirring gently to coat fruit. Arrange figs, cut sides up, in a single layer on a foil-lined baking sheet. Sprinkle figs evenly with 1/8 teaspoon ground cinnamon and 1/8 teaspoon salt. Bake at 350° for 10 minutes or until the fig juices begin to bubble. Remove from oven, and cool completely.
6. Combine 2 tablespoons honey and yogurt in a small bowl. Spoon 1/2 cup yogurt mixture into each of 6 bowls; top each serving with about 2 1/2 tablespoons granola and 6 fig quarters.

Note: You can store the granola in an airtight container in your pantry for up to 1 week or in the refrigerator for up to 1 month.

SERVES 6 (SERVING SIZE: 1 PARFAIT)
CALORIES 277; FAT 5.6G (SAT 0.6G, MONO 2.9G, POLY 1.8G); PROTEIN 13G; CARB 46G; FIBER 4G; CHOL 0MG; IRON 1MG; SODIUM 152MG; CALC 117MG

MORE IDEAS

How else can you serve these honeyed figs? Make them as a topping for a dessert pizza made with fresh Homemade Mozzarella (page 120). Or skip the vanilla and sugar, and top them with a dab of blue cheese.

homemade MOZZARELLA

HANDS-ON TIME: 19 MIN. TOTAL TIME: 49 MIN.

Making mozzarella is an art, but we've got a brilliant shortcut. It starts with fresh mozzarella cheese curds, found at most specialty cheese stores or ordered online. Mozzarella loses a lot of moisture during the stretching process, which can lead to tough cheese. That's why keeping it submerged in the heated salted water is crucial to keeping it pliable and soft.

4   **quarts water**
1   **teaspoon kosher salt**
1½ **pounds fresh mozzarella cheese curds, cut into 1-inch cubes**

1. Heat 4 quarts water in a large Dutch oven over medium-high heat until a thermometer registers 170°. Stir in salt.
2. Place cheese curd cubes in a medium bowl. Add enough hot salted water to cover cubes, keeping remaining water at 170°. Let cubes stand 5 minutes or until beginning to soften. Drain about half of water from cubes into a medium bowl; set drained water aside.
3. Add additional hot (170°) salted water to cubes; let stand 5 minutes or until cubes can be blended into a single, soft and stretchy mass.
4. Using the handle of a wooden spoon, lift a portion of curd out of the salt water, allowing it to return to bowl, flowing and folding back on itself. Continue lifting and stretching curd until smooth and shiny, adding more hot (170°) salted water, as needed, to keep curd soft and pliable.
5. Using spoon handle, lift a portion of curd out of water into your hands to form a thick, flat ribbon, keeping most of curd submerged. Gently roll ribbon into a 3- to 4-inch ball, tucking in sides as you roll. Pinch ribbon to sever it from ball.
6. Place ball in reserved salted water. Repeat rolling procedure with remaining curd to form an additional 4 balls. Let balls stand in salted water 20 minutes. Serve at room temperature.

Note: Cover and store, submerged in salt water, in refrigerator up to 1 week.

SERVES 20 (SERVING SIZE: 1 OUNCE)
CALORIES 109; FAT 8.5G (SAT 5.3G, MONO 1.2G, POLY 0.8G); PROTEIN 6G; CARB 0G; FIBER 0G; CHOL 30MG; IRON 0MG; SODIUM 102MG; CALC 122MG

CAPRESE "SALSA" ZUCCHINI
with sea salt

HANDS-ON TIME: 15 MIN. TOTAL TIME: 15 MIN.

Confronted with a summer bounty of zucchini? Make this grilled zucchini salad with a basil salsa and your Homemade Mozzarella. It's easily doubled or tripled. For more tender zucchini, leave the slices in the pan an extra 1 minute on each side. When the flesh looks translucent, the zucchini is done.

2   teaspoons extra-virgin olive oil
¼   teaspoon coarse sea salt
¼   teaspoon freshly ground black pepper
2   medium zucchini, cut diagonally into
      ½-inch-thick slices
⅓   cup diced tomato
2   ounces Homemade Mozzarella (page 120)
      or fresh mozzarella, sliced
3   tablespoons chopped fresh basil
1   garlic clove, minced
1   tablespoon extra-virgin olive oil
1   teaspoon red wine vinegar
Basil leaves (optional)

1. Preheat grill pan over medium-high heat.
2. Combine first 4 ingredients in a bowl; toss well to coat. Arrange zucchini in a single layer in pan; grill 4 minutes, turning after 2 minutes.
3. Combine tomato, mozzarella, basil, and minced garlic in a bowl. Add olive oil and red wine vinegar to tomato mixture; stir gently. Divide zucchini evenly among 4 plates. Top zucchini evenly with tomato salsa. Garnish with basil leaves, if desired.

SERVES 4

CALORIES 111; FAT 9.3G (SAT 2.8G, MONO 4.1G, POLY 0.7G); PROTEIN 4G; CARB 4G; FIBER 1G; CHOL 12MG; IRON 1MG; SODIUM 137MG; CALC 23MG

FLATBREAD
with pesto, mozzarella, tomato, and arugula

HANDS-ON TIME: 8 MIN. TOTAL TIME: 31 MIN.

Show off your Homemade Mozzarella with this quick pizza for four. Spread the flatbread with a layer of pesto, cheese, and roasted grape tomatoes; top with arugula; and watch this built-in salad pizza become a regular weeknight meal.

2 cups halved grape tomatoes
1 tablespoon olive oil, divided
4 (2-ounce) flatbreads
1/4 cup Pesto (page 168) or refrigerated reduced-fat pesto
4 ounces Homemade Mozzarella (page 120) or fresh mozzarella, shredded
4 cups loosely packed baby arugula leaves
1/8 teaspoon crushed red pepper (optional)

1. Preheat oven to 400°.
2. Combine grape tomatoes and 1 teaspoon olive oil, tossing to coat. Place tomatoes in a single layer on a jelly-roll pan. Bake at 400° for 10 minutes or until softened. Reduce oven temperature to 375°.
3. Place flatbreads on 2 baking sheets. Bake at 375° for 5 minutes or until beginning to crisp.

Spread 1 tablespoon pesto on each flatbread. Sprinkle each with 1/4 cup mozzarella cheese and 1/2 cup roasted tomatoes. Bake at 375° for 8 minutes or until cheese is melted and bubbly.

4. While flatbreads bake, combine arugula and 2 teaspoons olive oil, tossing well. Top flatbreads evenly with arugula. Sprinkle with crushed red pepper, if desired.

SERVES 4 (SERVING SIZE: 1 TOPPED FLATBREAD)

CALORIES 317; FAT 17G (SAT 5.5G, MONO 8.1G, POLY 2.1G); PROTEIN 15G; CARB 30G; FIBER 5G; CHOL 27MG; IRON 2MG; SODIUM 469MG; CALC 90MG

meatball SUBS

HANDS-ON TIME: 29 MIN. TOTAL TIME: 29 MIN.

If you're a fan of sub shops, you'll adore this favorite filled with tender meatballs, marinara sauce, roasted peppers, and grilled onions. Placing the sandwich under the broiler gets the top layer of mozzarella hot, beautifully brown, and deliciously melty. The secret to rolling meatballs is to wet your hands. This prevents the meat mixture from sticking to your hands. Roll the meatballs gently and form a light ball—rolling them too tightly can make them tough.

⅓ cup panko (Japanese breadcrumbs)
¼ teaspoon salt
¼ teaspoon crushed red pepper
12 ounces ground sirloin
3 garlic cloves, minced
1 large egg
Cooking spray
2 yellow bell peppers, halved and seeded
1⅓ cups lower-sodium marinara sauce or Slow-Cooker Marinara (page 257)
¾ cup vertically sliced onion
4 (2-ounce) hoagie sandwich buns
2 ounces Homemade Mozzarella (page 120) or fresh mozzarella cheese, thinly sliced
Basil leaves (optional)

1. Preheat broiler to high.
2. Combine first 6 ingredients in a bowl; mix gently. Working with damp hands, gently shape beef mixture into 16 meatballs. Arrange meatballs in a single layer on a heavy-duty baking sheet coated with cooking spray, leaving 6 inches of open space on one end. Place bell pepper halves, skin sides up, on open space on pan. Broil 6 inches from heat 7 minutes, turning meatballs once. Remove pan from oven. Place peppers in a small paper bag; fold to close tightly. Let stand 10 minutes. Remove peppers from bag. Peel and slice into ¼-inch-thick strips.
3. Bring marinara sauce to a simmer in a large skillet over medium-low heat; add meatballs, tossing to coat. Keep warm.
4. Heat a grill pan over medium-high heat; coat pan with cooking spray. Add onion; cook 6 minutes or until charred. Remove onion from pan.
5. Coat insides of buns with cooking spray, and broil 2 minutes or until toasted. Top each bun with 4 meatballs and ⅓ cup sauce. Divide peppers, onions, and cheese evenly among sandwiches; broil sandwiches open-faced 2 minutes or until cheese is bubbly and browned. Garnish with basil, if desired.

SERVES 4 (SERVING SIZE: 1 SUB)

CALORIES 423; FAT 16G (SAT 6.2G, MONO 5.6G, POLY 1.7G); PROTEIN 26G; CARB 44G; FIBER 5G; CHOL 100MG; IRON 4MG; SODIUM 708MG; CALC 107MG

homemade QUESO FRESCO

When baked into your favorite enchiladas or burritos, this lighter take on the ever-popular crumbly Mexican cheese will delight your diners with its rich, salty flavor and creamy texture. Try crumbling it over green salads or including it in mixed-grain salads for a soft, savory element.

2   quarts 1% low-fat milk
1   tablespoon kosher salt
3   tablespoons white vinegar

1. Bring milk and salt to a boil in a large Dutch oven over medium heat, stirring often. Reduce heat to low; add vinegar. Cook, stirring constantly, 2 to 4 minutes or until curds form.

2. Drain curds in a cheesecloth-lined sieve over a bowl. Let stand 20 minutes or until cool enough to handle. Gather corners of cheesecloth together, and twist to squeeze out excess moisture. Release corners of cheesecloth, and return curds and cheesecloth to sieve; cover and drain 1 hour.

Note: Wrap cheese in plastic wrap, and store in refrigerator up to 1 week.

SERVES 8 (SERVING SIZE: 1 OUNCE)
CALORIES 54; FAT 1.7G (SAT 1.1G, MONO 0.5G, POLY 0.1G); PROTEIN 7G; CARB 3G; FIBER 0G; CHOL 9MG; IRON 0MG; SODIUM 198MG; CALC 220MG

TECHNIQUE

Making Queso Fresco

1. Watch the milk carefully. The curds will form almost immediately. If not, add a little more vinegar. Acid makes the milk thicken to form curds.

2. If you prefer a drier cheese, press cheese between 2 flat plates after the 1-hour draining time. Weight the top with heavy cans. Let stand in refrigerator several hours or overnight.

STEP 1

STEP 2

blackened shrimp
TACOS

HANDS-ON TIME: 32 MIN. TOTAL TIME: 32 MIN.

A tangy sauce with Homemade Queso Fresco adds richness to these Cajun-style shrimp tacos. The tacos come together easily and make good use of your homemade Corn Tortillas, too.

2 tablespoons buttermilk

2 tablespoons canola mayonnaise or Homemade Mayonnaise (page 176)

½ teaspoon minced fresh garlic

½ teaspoon white vinegar

2 ounces Homemade Queso Fresco (page 128), crumbled (about ½ cup)

2 teaspoons paprika

1½ teaspoons ground cumin

¾ teaspoon garlic powder

½ teaspoon dried oregano

¼ teaspoon salt

¼ teaspoon dried thyme

¼ teaspoon ground red pepper

1 pound medium shrimp, peeled and deveined

Cooking spray

8 (6-inch) corn tortillas or Corn Tortillas (page 108)

½ cup diced plum tomato

1 ripe avocado, peeled and roughly mashed

Cilantro leaves (optional)

1. Combine first 5 ingredients in a small bowl; set sauce aside.
2. Combine paprika and next 6 ingredients (through ground red pepper) in a large zip-top plastic bag. Add shrimp to bag; seal and shake well to coat. Remove shrimp.
3. Heat a grill pan over high heat. Coat pan with cooking spray. Add shrimp; cook 2 minutes per side or until done.
4. Working with 1 tortilla at a time, heat tortillas over medium-high heat directly on the eye of a burner about 15 seconds on each side or until lightly charred. (You can also do this in the grill pan, if you like.) Divide shrimp evenly among tortillas; divide tomato, avocado, and sauce evenly among tacos. Serve with fresh cilantro, if desired.

SERVES 4 (SERVING SIZE: 2 TACOS)
CALORIES 287; FAT 13.5G (SAT 2.1G, MONO 6.6G, POLY 2.4G); PROTEIN 18G; CARB 27G; FIBER 6G; CHOL 120MG; IRON 1MG; SODIUM 372MG; CALC 130MG

homemade RICOTTA CHEESE

HANDS-ON TIME: 40 MIN. TOTAL TIME: 1 HR. 20 MIN.

Once you've tried fresh homemade ricotta, you'll find it hard to go back to the grocery store tubs. Serve it on crostini with Red Tomato Chutney (page 153) or drizzled with honey and chopped dried figs.

1 gallon 2% reduced-fat milk
5 cups low-fat buttermilk
½ teaspoon fine sea salt

1. Line a large colander or sieve with 5 layers of dampened cheesecloth, allowing the cheesecloth to extend outside edges of colander; place colander in a large bowl.
2. Combine milk and buttermilk in a large, heavy stockpot. Attach a candy thermometer to edge of pan so that thermometer extends at least 2 inches into milk mixture. Cook over medium-high heat until candy thermometer registers 170° (about 20 minutes), gently stirring occasionally. As soon as milk mixture reaches 170°, stop stirring (whey and curds will begin separating at this point). Continue to cook, without stirring, until the thermometer registers 190°. (Be sure not to stir, or curds that have formed will break apart.) Immediately remove pan from heat. (Bottom of pan may be slightly scorched.)
3. Using a slotted spoon, gently spoon curds into cheesecloth-lined colander; discard whey, or reserve it for another use. Drain over bowl 5 minutes. Gather edges of cheesecloth together; tie securely. Hang cheesecloth bundle from kitchen faucet; drain 15 minutes or until whey stops dripping. Scrape ricotta into a bowl. Sprinkle with salt; toss gently with a fork to combine. Cool to room temperature.

Note: This recipe yields 4 cups. Store in refrigerator up to 4 days.

SERVES 16 (SERVING SIZE: ¼ CUP)
CALORIES 79; FAT 4.5G (SAT 2.9G, MONO 1.3G, POLY 0.2G); PROTEIN 8G; CARB 1MG; FIBER 0G; CHOL 17MG; IRON 0MG; SODIUM 48MG; CALC 254MG

◇◇◇◇ TECHNIQUE ◇◇◇◇

Making Ricotta

1. An acid source is a requirement when making homemade ricotta. Without it, the milk won't thicken to form curds. Here, it comes from buttermilk, which is cultured with lactic acid bacteria.

2. As the milk mixture heats to 170°, be sure to stir gently and occasionally. If you stir too vigorously or too frequently (more than every few minutes), the curds may not separate as effectively from the whey.

3. Spoon the curds into a cheesecloth-lined colander to drain.

4. If your kitchen sink has a gooseneck faucet, it might be difficult to hang the cheesecloth bag on it. If so, lay a long wooden spoon across one corner of the sink, and hang the bag on the handle.

STEP 1

STEP 2

STEP 3

STEP 4

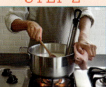

vanilla bean
ICE CREAM

HANDS-ON TIME: 23 MIN. TOTAL TIME: 4 HR. 30 MIN.

Our version of classic vanilla bean ice cream has 75 percent less fat than regular ice cream, but it's still rich, thanks to half-and-half, egg yolks, and one secret ingredient: evaporated low-fat milk. With 60 percent of the water removed, it yields fewer ice crystals and a creamier texture. Vanilla beans scraped from the pod add flavor and the little specks that give vanilla ice cream its characteristic look.

1 cup half-and-half
½ cup sugar, divided
2 tablespoons light-colored corn syrup
⅛ teaspoon salt
1 (12-ounce) can evaporated low-fat milk
1 vanilla bean, split lengthwise
3 large egg yolks

1. Combine half-and-half, ¼ cup sugar, corn syrup, salt, and evaporated milk in a medium heavy saucepan. Scrape seeds from vanilla bean; add seeds and bean to milk mixture. Heat milk mixture to 180° or until tiny bubbles form around edge (do not boil). Remove pan from heat; cover and let stand 10 minutes.

2. Combine ¼ cup sugar and egg yolks in a medium bowl, stirring well with a whisk. Gradually add hot milk mixture to egg mixture, stirring constantly with a whisk. Return milk mixture to pan. Cook over medium heat until a thermometer registers 160°, stirring constantly. Remove from heat.

3. Place pan in a large ice-filled bowl for 20 minutes or until egg mixture is cool, stirring occasionally. Pour milk mixture through a fine sieve into the freezer can of an ice-cream freezer; discard solids. Freeze according to manufacturer's instructions. Spoon ice cream into a freezer-safe container; cover and freeze 3 hours or until firm.

SERVES 8 (SERVING SIZE: ½ CUP)
CALORIES 161; FAT 5.9G (SAT 3.1G, MONO 1.9G, POLY 0.4G); PROTEIN 5G; CARB 23G; FIBER 0G; CHOL 88MG; IRON 0MG; SODIUM 108MG; CALC 161MG

CHOCOLATE TACOS
with ice cream and peanuts

HANDS-ON TIME: 11 MIN. TOTAL TIME: 62 MIN.

½ cup powdered sugar
1.1 ounces all-purpose flour (about ¼ cup)
3 tablespoons unsweetened cocoa
1 teaspoon cornstarch
¼ teaspoon salt
3 tablespoons egg whites
1 teaspoon 2% reduced-fat milk
¼ teaspoon vanilla extract
Cooking spray
½ cup semisweet chocolate chips
1 teaspoon canola oil
½ cup finely chopped unsalted, dry-roasted peanuts, divided
2⅔ cups Vanilla Bean Ice Cream (page 136) or low-fat vanilla ice cream

1. Preheat oven to 400°.
2. Combine first 5 ingredients, stirring well. Stir in egg whites, milk, and vanilla.
3. Coat a baking sheet with cooking spray. Using your finger, draw 4 (5-inch) circles on baking sheet. Spoon 1 tablespoon batter onto each circle, spreading to edges of circle. Bake at 400° for 6 minutes or until edges begin to brown. Loosen edges with a spatula; remove from baking sheet. Working quickly, gently drape each circle over suspended wooden spoons, gently shaping into a shell; cool completely. (Shells are delicate.) Repeat procedure to form a total of 8 shells.
4. Combine chocolate chips and oil in a small microwave-safe bowl. Microwave at HIGH 1 minute or until chocolate melts, stirring after 30 seconds; stir until smooth. Gently spread about 1 teaspoon chocolate sauce on the top third of the outside of both sides of cooled shells; sprinkle with about 1 teaspoon chopped peanuts. Spoon ice cream into each shell. Drizzle remaining chocolate sauce over ice cream; sprinkle with remaining peanuts. Freeze for at least 30 minutes before serving.

SERVES 8 (SERVING SIZE: 1 TACO)
CALORIES 233; FAT 11.8G (SAT 4G, MONO 2.6G, POLY 1.6G); PROTEIN 7G; CARB 33G; FIBER 5G; CHOL 3MG; IRON 1MG; SODIUM 121MG; CALC 73MG

TECHNIQUE

Making Chocolate Taco Shells

1. Drawing circles in the cooking spray helps contain the chocolate mixture, preventing it from spreading and yielding the perfect-sized taco shell.

2. This is a small amount of batter, so be sure to spread the mixture evenly, which will create a thin taco.

3. Loosen the edges very gently to avoid breakage.

4. When shaping the shells, balance the wooden spoons between objects that are about 6 inches apart.

STEP 1

STEP 2

STEP 3

STEP 4

chocolate fudge brownie
ICE CREAM

HANDS-ON TIME: 30 MIN. TOTAL TIME: 2 HR.

Brownies:

1/2 ounce bittersweet chocolate, chopped

1/2 cup sugar

2 tablespoons butter, softened

1/2 teaspoon vanilla extract

1 large egg, lightly beaten

2.25 ounces all-purpose flour (about 1/2 cup)

1/3 cup unsweetened cocoa

1/4 teaspoon baking powder

1/8 teaspoon salt

Cooking spray

Ice cream:

1 1/3 cups sugar

1/3 cup unsweetened cocoa

3 1/2 cups 2% reduced-fat milk, divided

3 large egg yolks

1/2 cup half-and-half

2 1/2 ounces bittersweet chocolate, chopped

1. Preheat oven to 350°.
2. To prepare brownies, place 1/2 ounce chocolate in a microwave-safe dish, and microwave at HIGH 30 seconds or until almost melted, stirring once. Combine chocolate, 1/2 cup sugar, and butter in a medium bowl; beat with a mixer at high speed until well blended. Add extract and egg; beat until combined. Weigh or lightly spoon flour into a dry measuring cup; level with a knife. Combine flour, 1/3 cup cocoa, baking powder, and salt. Add flour mixture to sugar mixture; beat just until blended. Spoon batter into a 9 x 5–inch loaf pan coated with cooking spray. Bake at 350° for 20 minutes or until a wooden pick inserted in the center comes out clean. Cool in pan on a wire rack.
3. To prepare ice cream, combine 1 1/3 cups sugar and 1/3 cup cocoa in a medium, heavy saucepan over medium-low heat, stirring well with a whisk. Stir in 1/2 cup milk and egg yolks. Stir in 3 cups milk. Cook 12 minutes or until a thermometer registers 160°, stirring constantly. Remove from heat.
4. Place half-and-half in a medium microwave-safe bowl; microwave at high 1 1/2 minutes or until half-and-half boils. Add 2 1/2 ounces chocolate; stir until smooth. Stir half-and-half mixture into milk mixture. Place pan in a large ice-filled bowl. Cool completely, stirring occasionally.
5. Pour mixture into the freezer can of an ice-cream freezer; freeze according to manufacturer's instructions. Spoon ice cream into a freezer-safe container. Cut brownies into small squares; stir into ice cream. Cover and freeze 1 hour or until firm.

SERVES 14 (SERVING SIZE: ABOUT 1/2 CUP)
CALORIES 233; FAT 7.5G (SAT 4G, MONO 2.4G, POLY 0.4G); PROTEIN 5G; CARB 39G; FIBER 2G; CHOL 71MG; IRON 1MG; SODIUM 83MG; CALC 29MG

Chapter 5

JAMS, SPREADS & CONDIMENTS

There's something refreshingly old-fashioned and rewarding about putting up jams and making your own condiments and salad dressings. Contrary to what you might imagine, it doesn't involve a truckload of produce, sterilized jars, or a weekend spent in the kitchen.

You can make all these jams, spreads, and condiments in small amounts, often by just stirring ingredients together or cooking them for a short time. Many of the recipes are easily doubled or tripled, making them ideal to fill your pantry or take to a holiday meal.

With an eye toward peak seasonal freshness, you'll want to make jams, pesto, ketchup, and Green Goddess dressing during the summer. Wait for fall when fresh cranberries are ripe to prepare cranberry sauce. The rest are made with ingredients sold year-round. Nuts are always available for rich nut butters, as are dried fruits for Apricot-Fig Chutney (page 150) and frozen fruit for Warm Berry Compote (page 155). And you'll notice many of the recipes contain reduced amounts of sugar, corn syrup, and sodium compared to packaged equivalents, but still with delicious results.

Concord
GRAPE JAM

HANDS-ON TIME: 32 MIN. TOTAL TIME: 4 HR. 12 MIN.

Spread this flavorful refrigerator jam over warm homemade Buttermilk Biscuits (page 37) for a simple breakfast. Usually found only at farmers' markets, Concord grapes have a full, intense flavor. They are a slip-skin variety, which means the skins can be pinched off easily.

3   pounds fresh Concord grapes, stemmed (about 8 cups)
³⁄₄   cup sugar, divided
2   teaspoons grated lemon rind
4   teaspoons fresh lemon juice

1. Pinch grapes to separate pulp from skins. Place skins in a bowl; set aside. Place grape pulp and ¼ cup sugar in a medium sauce-pan; bring to a boil. Reduce heat; simmer 10 minutes or until seeds begin to separate from pulp.
2. Press pulp mixture through a fine sieve into a bowl. Discard seeds. Place skins, ½ cup sugar, rind, juice, and pulp in saucepan; bring to a boil. Reduce heat; simmer until reduced to 2½ cups (about 2 hours and 45 minutes), stirring occasionally. Pour into a bowl; cool.

Note: The recipe makes about 2½ cups jam. Store the jam in an airtight container in the refrigerator for up to 2 weeks.

SERVES 20 (SERVING SIZE: 2 TABLESPOONS)
CALORIES 56; FAT 0.1G (SAT 0.1G, MONO 0G, POLY 0G); PROTEIN 0G; CARB 14G; FIBER 0G; CHOL 0MG; IRON 0MG; SODIUM 1MG; CALC 6MG

fresh
STRAWBERRY JAM

HANDS-ON TIME: 7 MIN. TOTAL TIME: 2 HR. 7 MIN.

No need for pectin or canning techniques for this bright, fresh refrigerator jam. It comes together in a flash, once you've prepped the strawberries.

4   cups halved fresh strawberries
1   cup sugar
2   teaspoons fresh lemon juice

1. Combine strawberries and sugar in a medium saucepan, and bring to a simmer over medium-high heat, stirring frequently.
2. Reduce heat to medium, and simmer 1 hour or until thick, stirring occasionally.
3. Remove from heat, and stir in lemon juice. Cool to room temperature (about 1 hour).

Note: This recipe makes 2 cups jam. Store the jam in an airtight container in the refrigerator for up to 3 months.

SERVES 32 (SERVING SIZE: 1 TABLESPOON)
CALORIES 30; FAT 0.1G (SAT 0G, MONO 0G, POLY 0.1G); PROTEIN 0G; CARB 8G; FIBER 0G; CHOL 0MG; IRON 0MG; SODIUM 0MG; CALC 3MG

MORE IDEAS

What to do with strawberry jam besides spread it on toast or an English muffin? Top a torte (page 135), spread it between cake layers, swirl it into yogurt, top pancakes or waffles, or drop a spoonful into muffins for a sweet surprise.

LEMON CURD

HANDS-ON TIME: 10 MIN. TOTAL TIME: 1 HR. 10 MIN.

Lemon curd is a versatile topping, perfect with warm gingerbread, pound cake, muffins, or any number of sweet treats. For a lime variation, substitute lime rind and juice for the lemon rind and juice.

¾ cup sugar
1 tablespoon grated lemon rind
2 large eggs
⅔ cup fresh lemon juice (about 3 large lemons)
2 tablespoons butter

1. Combine first 3 ingredients in a medium saucepan over medium heat, stirring with a whisk. Cook until sugar dissolves and mixture is light in color (about 3 minutes). Stir in lemon juice and butter; cook 5 minutes or until mixture thinly coats the back of a spoon, stirring constantly with a whisk. Cool. Cover and chill 1 hour (the mixture will thicken as it cools).

Note: This recipe yields 1⅓ cups of lemon curd. It can be stored in an airtight container in the refrigerator for up to 1 month. You can easily double the recipe, and freeze half of it in a heavy-duty zip-top plastic bag for up to 6 months. Thaw in the refrigerator, and use within 1 month.

SERVES 21 (SERVING SIZE: ABOUT 1 TABLESPOON)

CALORIES 47; FAT 1.6G (SAT 0.8G, MONO 0.5G, POLY 0.1G); PROTEIN 1G; CARB 8G; FIBER 0G; CHOL 24MG; IRON 0MG; SODIUM 18MG; CALC 4MG

apricot-fig CHUTNEY

HANDS-ON TIME: 10 MIN. TOTAL TIME: 25 MIN.

Chutney is usually associated with Indian food, but its sweet and sour flavors work with lots of disparate dishes. You'll find a wide variety of uses for this tangy relish.

MORE IDEAS

This sweet, jammy relish works well on cheese and crackers, in chicken salad and dips, and mixed with canola mayonnaise as a spread for sandwiches and wraps. Add it to marinades, salad dressings, and tuna salad for a little kick.

3   cups peeled, pitted, and quartered apricots
½   cup dried figs, quartered
½   cup dry white wine
⅓   cup sugar
¼   cup golden raisins
1½   teaspoons chopped fresh thyme
1   tablespoon honey
1   tablespoon fresh lemon juice
1   teaspoon mustard seeds
½   teaspoon cumin
½   teaspoon ground ginger
¼   teaspoon kosher salt
Dash of ground red pepper
½   jalapeño, finely chopped
½   shallot, sliced
2   tablespoons chopped fresh cilantro

1. Combine all ingredients except cilantro in a large Dutch oven over medium heat, and simmer 15 minutes. Stir in cilantro.

Note: This recipe makes 2½ cups of chutney. If you're storing it for later use, omit the cilantro. Store the chutney in an airtight container in the refrigerator for up to 3 months. Stir in fresh cilantro just before serving.

SERVES 10 (SERVING SIZE: ¼ CUP)
CALORIES 99; FAT 0.4G (SAT 0G, MONO 0.2G, POLY 0.1G); PROTEIN 1G; CARB 24G; FIBER 2G; CHOL 0MG; IRON 1MG; SODIUM 61MG; CALC 24MG

red tomato CHUTNEY

HANDS-ON TIME: 55 MIN. TOTAL TIME: 1 HR. 55 MIN.

This sweet-tart chutney pairs summer tomatoes with dried cranberries, making it an all-purpose condiment for barbecues. Spoon it over burgers and grilled chicken. In cooler weather, toss a little chutney with roasted vegetables, such as parsnips, turnips, or sweet potatoes.

3 cups finely chopped peeled tomato (about 4 large)
1 cup finely chopped red bell pepper
1 cup finely chopped red onion
½ cup dried cranberries
½ cup cider vinegar
¼ cup granulated sugar
¼ cup packed brown sugar
2 tablespoons minced peeled fresh ginger
½ teaspoon salt
½ teaspoon mustard seeds
¼ teaspoon ground cinnamon
¼ teaspoon ground cumin
¼ teaspoon ground allspice
⅛ teaspoon ground red pepper

1. Combine all ingredients in a large saucepan; bring to a boil. Reduce heat, and simmer, uncovered, 45 minutes or until thick, stirring frequently. Cool; pour into airtight containers.

Note: Refrigerate in airtight containers up to 2 months.

SERVES 28 (SERVING SIZE: 2 TABLESPOONS)
CALORIES 30; FAT 0.1G (SAT 0G, MONO 0G, POLY 0.1G); PROTEIN 0G; CARB 8G; FIBER 1G; CHOL 0MG; IRON 0MG; SODIUM 44MG; CALC 6MG

warm berry COMPOTE

◇◇

HANDS-ON TIME: 8 MIN. TOTAL TIME: 8 MIN.

◇◇

If you're wondering what to serve company, this sugar-free compote makes a pretty topping for ice cream or angel food cake. Hints of cinnamon add a subtle flavor to the berries. Keep a bag of frozen mixed berries around for this last-minute treat. It's also great over pancakes, yogurt, or ricotta.

◇◇

1   teaspoon butter
2   tablespoons honey
2   teaspoons fresh lemon juice
Dash of ground cinnamon
1   (12-ounce) bag frozen mixed berries

1. Melt butter in a saucepan over medium heat. Add honey, lemon juice, a dash of ground cinnamon, and mixed berries; bring to a boil. Reduce heat; simmer 5 minutes.

Note: This recipe makes 1⅓ cups. Store the compote in an airtight container in the refrigerator for up to 1 week.

◇◇◇◇◇◇◇◇◇◇◇◇◇◇◇◇◇◇◇◇◇◇◇◇◇◇◇◇◇◇◇◇◇◇◇◇◇◇

SERVES 4 (SERVING SIZE: ⅓ CUP)
CALORIES 78; FAT 1.3G (SAT 0.6G, MONO 0.3G, POLY 0G); PROTEIN 1G; CARB 19G; FIBER 2G; CHOL 3MG; IRON 0MG; SODIUM 1MG; CALC 14MG

basic CRANBERRY SAUCE

HANDS-ON TIME: 14 MIN. TOTAL TIME: 1 HR. 31 MIN.

Impress your Thanksgiving guests with this tangy-sweet sauce, which cooks for only 12 minutes. Made with fresh cranberries, it pairs beautifully with chicken, quail, duck, or ham, as well as turkey, so no need to wait for a holiday.

MORE IDEAS

Sure, you can slather this sauce on the traditional post-Thanksgiving turkey sandwich, but you can go beyond the basic uses, too. Add it to barbecue sauce, warm it and spoon over cake or ice cream, or stir it into balsamic vinaigrette for a tangy, sweet dressing for bitter salad greens like arugula.

½   cup packed dark brown sugar
½   cup fresh orange juice (about 2 oranges)
¼   cup water
1½   tablespoons honey
⅛   teaspoon ground allspice
1   (12-ounce) package fresh cranberries
1   (3-inch) cinnamon stick

1. Combine all ingredients in a medium sauce-pan over medium-high heat; bring to a boil. Reduce heat, and simmer 12 minutes or until mixture is slightly thickened, stirring occasionally. Discard cinnamon stick; cool completely.

Note: The recipe yields 1¾ cups of sauce. Store it in an airtight container in the refrigerator for up to 2 months.

SERVES 14 (SERVING SIZE: 2 TABLESPOONS)
CALORIES 54; FAT 0G; PROTEIN 0G; CARB 14G; FIBER 1G; CHOL 0MG; IRON 0MG; SODIUM 3MG; CALC 8MG

caramelized ONION MARMALADE

HANDS-ON TIME: 10 MIN. TOTAL TIME: 50 MIN.

This marmalade makes a wonderful topping for bruschetta or pizza; it's also a nice complement to grilled flank steak, chicken, or pork. By covering the pan, you'll cut down the constant stirring required to caramelize the onions.

1   tablespoon butter
3   tablespoons brown sugar
10   cups thinly sliced sweet onions (about 4 large)
4   garlic cloves, minced
2   tablespoons red wine vinegar
¾   teaspoon salt
⅛   teaspoon freshly ground black pepper

1. Melt butter in a large nonstick skillet over medium heat. Add sugar to pan; cook 1 minute or until sugar dissolves. Add onions and garlic to pan. Cover and cook 30 minutes or until onions are very tender and browned, stirring occasionally.

2. Uncover and add vinegar to onion mixture. Cook, uncovered, 10 minutes or until the onions are deeply brown, stirring frequently. Stir in salt and pepper.

Note: This recipe yields 1½ cups. Store the marmalade in an airtight container in the refrigerator for up to 1 month.

SERVES 12 (SERVING SIZE: 2 TABLESPOONS)

CALORIES 44; FAT 1G (SAT 0.6G, MONO 0.3G, POLY 0.1G); PROTEIN 1G; CARB 9G; FIBER 1G; CHOL 3MG; IRON 0MG; SODIUM 157MG; CALC 16MG

STEP 1

STEP 2

STEP 3

STEP 4

TECHNIQUE

Caramelizing Onions

When caramelizing onions, don't rush: This transformation takes time. The hallmark of properly caramelized onions isn't just a richly browned exterior, but also a meltingly tender, almost jam-like texture and a taste that's as sweet as sugar.

1. After 15 minutes: The onions are beginning to brown, but they still have some crunch.

2. 20 minutes: The onions are nicely browned, but they need more time over the heat.

3. 25 minutes: The onions are richly browned, and you may be tempted to stop here, but give them more time. It's worth it.

4. 30 minutes: The onions are deeply browned, and the texture is sweetly jammy. They're ready.

homemade NUT BUTTERS

HANDS-ON TIME: VARIES TOTAL TIME: VARIES

Homemade nut butters taste better but are more perishable than commercial varieties, so it's best to make them in small batches. Buy roasted nuts, rather than raw, to heighten the flavor—or roast the nuts yourself. As a general rule, figure on a ratio of 2-to-1 of nuts to nut butter. (For example, 1 cup of nuts will make ¹/₂ cup of nut butter). In each of the recipes below, we started with 2 cups of nuts. Place the nuts in a food processor, and process until they form a paste. Some nut butters will be creamy; others a bit grainy. The higher the fat, the smoother the nut butter. You can store homemade butters covered in the refrigerator for up to 1 month.

Peanut Butter

Use plain roasted peanuts rather than dry-roasted, which are seasoned with paprika, garlic, and onion powder. This smooth nut butter has a distinctive fresh peanut flavor, and the nuts take about 2 minutes to process.

SERVES 16 (SERVING SIZE: 1 TABLESPOON)
CALORIES 94; FAT 8.1G (SAT 1.7G); SODIUM 0MG

Cashew Butter

This smooth butter forms in about 2 minutes of processing. It's a good substitute for tahini. Use either roasted or raw cashews.

SERVES 16 (SERVING SIZE: 1 TABLESPOON)
CALORIES 94; FAT 7.9G (SAT 1.6G); SODIUM 0MG

Almond Butter

Slivered roasted almonds take about 3¹/₂ minutes to form a butter, but roasted whole almonds have additional oil and will be ready in just 2¹/₂ minutes.

SERVES 16 (SERVING SIZE: 1 TABLESPOON)
CALORIES 98; FAT 8.9G (SAT 0.7G); SODIUM 0MG

Walnut Butter

Like pecan butter, this soft, oily butter is ready in about a minute. It, too, has a bitter aftertaste from the skins, making it better for recipes than sandwiches. Roasted walnut halves are expensive, so look for pieces.

SERVES 16 (SERVING SIZE: 1 TABLESPOON)
CALORIES 100; FAT 10G (SAT 1G); SODIUM 0MG

Macadamia Butter

Roasted macadamias, which have a high fat content, grind into butter in just 2 minutes, but it's too thin to immediately spread on bread. Chill this nut butter to thicken it.

◇◇◇◇◇◇◇◇◇◇◇◇◇◇◇◇◇◇◇◇◇◇◇◇◇◇◇◇◇◇

SERVES 16 (SERVING SIZE: 1 TABLESPOON)

CALORIES 115; FAT 12G (SAT 2G); SODIUM 0MG

Pecan Butter

Roasted pecans process into rich butter in about a minute. The loose paste spreads easily, but the skins give it a slightly bitter aftertaste, which makes it better for recipes than sandwiches.

◇◆◇◇◇◇◇◇◇◇◇◇◇◇◇◇◇◇◇◇◇◇◇◇◇◇◇◇◇◇◇

SERVES 16 (SERVING SIZE: 1 TABLESPOON)

CALORIES 98; FAT 10G (SAT 1G); SODIUM 0MG

Hazelnut Butter

This grainy, thick butter with brown specks is fruity and naturally sweet. Processing it takes about 2½ minutes. If the nuts are whole, toast them in a 400° oven for 5 minutes or until they start to look shiny and the skins begin to loosen. Rub the nuts in a dishtowel to remove skins.

◇◇◇◇◇◇◇◇◇◇◇◇◇◇◇◇◇◇◇◇◇◇◇◇◇◇◇◇◇◇◇

SERVES 16 (SERVING SIZE: 1 TABLESPOON)
CALORIES 90; FAT 8G (SAT 0.5G); SODIUM 0MG

Pistachio Butter

Roasted ground pistachios make a very dry, crumbly butter that is best combined with something else, like softened cream cheese. It takes 3½ to 4 minutes to grind into butter, and it tends to clump during processing.

◇◇◇◇◇◇◇◇◇◇◇◇◇◇◇◇◇◇◇◇◇◇◇◇◇◇◇◇◇◇◇

SERVES 16 (SERVING SIZE: 1 TABLESPOON)
CALORIES 90; FAT 6.5G (SAT 0.8G); SODIUM 0MG

CHOCOLATE-HAZELNUT
spread

HANDS-ON TIME: 6 MIN. TOTAL TIME: 21 MIN.

Making your own homemade chocolate-hazelnut spread that mimics the addictive qualities of the store-bought variety is easy to do. Just keep in mind that it has sugar, while nut butters do not.

1½ cups hazelnuts
¾ cup powdered sugar
⅓ cup Dutch process cocoa
¼ cup canola oil
½ teaspoon vanilla extract
¼ teaspoon salt
½ cup plus 1 tablespoon boiling water

1. Preheat oven to 350°.
2. Place hazelnuts on a baking sheet. Bake at 350° for 15 minutes, stirring once. Turn nuts out onto a dish towel. Roll up towel; rub off skins.

3. Place hazelnuts in a food processor; process 1 minute or until a paste forms. Add powdered sugar and next 4 ingredients (through salt), and process 1 to 2 minutes or until blended. With processor on, gradually add boiling water through food chute, processing until smooth.

Note: Store the spread in an airtight container in the refrigerator for up to 2 weeks.

SERVES 32 (SERVING SIZE: 1 TABLESPOON)
CALORIES 70; FAT 5.7G (SAT 0.4G, MONO 4G, POLY 1G); PROTEIN 1G; CARB 4G; FIBER 1G; CHOL 0MG; IRON 1MG; SODIUM 19MG; CALC 7MG

MORE IDEAS

What doesn't taste good with this spread on it? Slather on bread or dip breadsticks and strawberries into it. Top banana slices with it, bake it into thumbprint cookies, or use as the filling for sandwich cookies.

chocolate-hazelnut
FRENCH TOAST SANDWICHES

HANDS-ON TIME: 15 MIN. TOTAL TIME: 17 MIN.

For a dessert-like breakfast or brunch, try this French toast stuffed with homemade Chocolate-Hazelnut Spread. You put the spread on the bread first, make a sandwich, and then dip it in the milk mixture before cooking in a skillet. Topped with strawberries and powdered sugar, it's pretty enough to serve to guests.

2   cups sliced fresh strawberries
3   tablespoons granulated sugar, divided
1¼   cups 1% low-fat milk
3   large eggs
9   tablespoons Chocolate-Hazelnut Spread (page 165)
12   (¾-ounce) slices diagonally cut French bread (about ¾ inch thick)
Cooking spray
2   teaspoons powdered sugar

1. Combine strawberries and 1 tablespoon granulated sugar in a small bowl. Let stand while preparing French toast, stirring occasionally to release juice.

2. Combine milk, 2 tablespoons granulated sugar, and eggs in a shallow dish, stirring with a whisk.

3. Spread 1½ tablespoons Chocolate-Hazelnut Spread on each of 6 bread slices; top with remaining 6 slices, pressing gently. Working with 1 sandwich at a time, dip sandwich in milk mixture; let stand 1 minute on each side. Transfer sandwich to a large plate. Repeat procedure with 2 more sandwiches.

4. Heat a large nonstick skillet over medium-high heat. Coat dipped sandwiches with cooking spray. Add sandwiches to pan; cook 1 to 2 minutes on each side or until browned. Remove from pan; keep warm.

5. While first 3 sandwiches cook, repeat soaking procedure with remaining 3 sandwiches. Add remaining 3 sandwiches to pan; cook 1 to 2 minutes or until browned. Dust sandwiches evenly with powdered sugar, and top evenly with sugared strawberries.

SERVES 6 (SERVING SIZE: 1 FRENCH TOAST SANDWICH, ⅓ TEASPOON POWDERED SUGAR, AND ⅓ CUP SUGARED STRAWBERRIES)

CALORIES 333; FAT 12.7G (SAT 2G, MONO 7.5G, POLY 2.5G); PROTEIN 12G; CARB 45G; FIBER 3G; CHOL 96MG; IRON 3MG; SODIUM 305MG; CALC 116MG

PESTO

Got a food processor? If so, it only takes a few moments to whip up a fresh batch of pesto. Make multiple batches in summertime, when basil leaves are fat and bushy plants grow in abundance. Warm water cuts the amount of olive oil needed to make a paste.

MORE IDEAS

Pesto is endlessly versatile and a quick way to add a blast of flavor to your food. Thin it and brush it onto grilled fish, mix it with mayonnaise for a sandwich spread, use it as a base for your pizza in place of tomato sauce, or spoon it into a bowl of minestrone or chowder.

You can also spoon it on homemade pasta (page 87) or Ravioli with Herbed Ricotta Filling (page 89) or dip Cheesy Herb Breadsticks (page 82) in it.

4   garlic cloves, peeled
4   cups packed basil leaves (about 2½ ounces)
¼   cup pine nuts
2   ounces grated fresh Parmesan cheese (½ cup)
¾   teaspoon salt
½   teaspoon freshly ground black pepper
½   cup warm water
6   tablespoons extra-virgin olive oil

1. Drop garlic through food chute with food processor on; process until minced. Place basil and next 4 ingredients (through black pepper) in processor; process 10 seconds.

2. Combine ½ cup warm water and oil in a measuring cup. With processor on, slowly pour oil mixture through food chute, processing just until blended.

Note: When storing, cover the surface of the pesto with plastic wrap to prevent discoloration. It should keep for up to 2 weeks in the refrigerator in a sealed container or up to 3 months in the freezer.

SERVES 20 (SERVING SIZE: 1 TABLESPOON)
CALORIES 59; FAT 5.7G (SAT 1.2G, MONO 3.5G, POLY 0.7G); PROTEIN 2G; CARB 1G; FIBER 0G; CHOL 2MG; IRON 0MG; SODIUM 134MG; CALC 41MG

spinach-herb pesto
LINGUINE

HANDS-ON TIME: 19 MIN. TOTAL TIME: 28 MIN.

Baby spinach takes the place of most of the usual basil to give the pesto an earthy flavor. The thick, emerald sauce coats the flat noodles beautifully and serves up an herb bouquet of basil, oregano, and thyme in every forkful.

4   ounces fresh baby spinach
¼   cup slivered blanched almonds
¼   cup basil leaves
2   teaspoons chopped fresh oregano
1   teaspoon chopped fresh thyme
¼   teaspoon freshly ground black pepper
1   large garlic clove, chopped
2   tablespoons organic vegetable broth
2   teaspoons fresh lemon juice
¼   teaspoon salt
2   tablespoons extra-virgin olive oil
1   ounce Parmigiano-Reggiano cheese, grated and divided (about ¼ cup)
8   ounces uncooked linguine

1. Place spinach in a microwave-safe bowl; cover bowl with plastic wrap. Microwave at HIGH 2 minutes or until spinach wilts. Remove plastic wrap; cool slightly.

2. Place spinach, almonds, and next 5 ingredients (through garlic) in a food processor. Process until chopped. Add broth, juice, and salt; pulse 5 times. With processor on, slowly pour oil through food chute; process until well blended. Scrape into a bowl; stir in half of cheese. Cover pesto with plastic wrap.

3. Cook pasta according to package directions, omitting salt and fat. Drain. Toss pasta with ½ cup pesto. Arrange about 1½ cups pasta mixture in each of 4 bowls; top each serving with 2 tablespoons remaining pesto and 1½ teaspoons remaining cheese.

SERVES 4
CALORIES 353; FAT 13.2G (SAT 2.6G, MONO 7.7G, POLY 1.8G); PROTEIN 13G; CARB 48G; FIBER 4G; CHOL 5MG; IRON 3MG; SODIUM 327MG; CALC 145MG

homemade BASIC MUSTARD

HANDS-ON TIME: 5 MIN. TOTAL TIME: 2 DAYS

The success of homemade mustard depends on the freshness of the mustard seeds. If you can't find mustard seeds at the supermarket, try Indian markets. Be sure to mix these together in a nonreactive bowl (like glass or stainless steel) to avoid off flavors from the acid interacting with metal.

6   tablespoons yellow mustard seeds
$\frac{1}{3}$ cup dry white wine
$\frac{1}{3}$ cup white wine vinegar
$\frac{1}{2}$ teaspoon salt
$\frac{1}{8}$ teaspoon ground red pepper
$\frac{1}{3}$ cup water

1. Combine first 5 ingredients in a glass, stainless steel, or other nonreactive bowl. Cover and refrigerate 2 days.
2. Place mustard seed mixture in a blender; process until smooth, adding water as needed for desired consistency.

Note: Store the mustard in an airtight container in the refrigerator for up to 1 month.

SERVES 20 (SERVING SIZE: 1 TABLESPOON)
CALORIES 17; FAT 0.8G (SAT 0G, MONO 0.6G, POLY 0.2G); PROTEIN 1G; CARB 1G; FIBER 0G; CHOL 0MG; IRON 0MG; SODIUM 60MG; CALC 18MG

Grainy Mustard

Combine $\frac{2}{3}$ cup dry white wine, 3 tablespoons yellow mustard seeds, 3 tablespoons brown mustard seeds, 1 tablespoon minced shallots, $\frac{1}{2}$ teaspoon salt, and $\frac{1}{8}$ teaspoon ground turmeric in a glass, stainless steel, or other nonreactive bowl. Cover and refrigerate 2 days. Place mustard mixture and 1 teaspoon prepared horseradish in a blender; process until coarsely ground. Transfer to a glass jar. Cover and store in refrigerator for up to 1 month.

SERVES 16 (SERVING SIZE: 1 TABLESPOON)
CALORIES 26; FAT 1G (SAT 0G, MONO 0.8G, POLY 0.2G); PROTEIN 1G; CARB 2G; FIBER 1G; CHOL 0MG; IRON 0MG; SODIUM 76MG; CALC 24MG

Honey Mustard

Combine $\frac{1}{2}$ cup cider vinegar, $\frac{1}{4}$ cup honey, 3 tablespoons yellow mustard seeds, 3 tablespoons brown mustard seeds, $\frac{1}{2}$ teaspoon salt, $\frac{1}{8}$ teaspoon ground turmeric, and $\frac{1}{8}$ teaspoon ground red pepper in a glass, stainless steel, or other nonreactive bowl. Cover and refrigerate 2 days. Place mustard mixture in a blender; process until smooth. Transfer to a glass jar. Cover and store in refrigerator for up to 1 month.

SERVES 18 (SERVING SIZE: 1 TABLESPOON)
CALORIES 31; FAT 0.9G (SAT 0G, MONO 0.7G, POLY 0.2G); PROTEIN 1G; CARB 5G; FIBER 1G; CHOL 0MG; IRON 0MG; SODIUM 67MG; CALC 21MG

heirloom tomato
KETCHUP

HANDS-ON TIME: 23 MIN. TOTAL TIME: 1 HR. 28 MIN.

Both store-bought and homemade ketchup contain lycopene, an antioxidant associated with decreased risk of chronic diseases. We found this rendition well worth making because it captures the vibrant flavor of summer tomatoes and has about half the sodium of regular ketchup.

½   teaspoon yellow mustard seeds
½   teaspoon celery seeds
¼   teaspoon whole allspice
¼   teaspoon black peppercorns
2   garlic cloves, chopped
3   pounds heirloom tomatoes, cut into chunks (about 4½ cups)
2   cups chopped onion (1 medium)
1   cup chopped red bell pepper (1 small)
⅓   cup cider vinegar
1   tablespoon sugar
½   teaspoon salt

1. Place mustard seeds, celery seeds, allspice, and peppercorns on a double layer of cheesecloth. Gather edges of cheesecloth together; tie securely.

2. Combine cheesecloth bag, garlic, tomatoes, and next 3 ingredients (through vinegar) in a large Dutch oven; bring to a boil. Cover, reduce heat, and simmer 20 minutes. Transfer to a bowl. Remove cheesecloth bag, and set aside.

3. Place half of tomato mixture in a blender. Remove center piece of blender lid (to allow steam to escape); secure blender lid on blender. Place a clean towel over opening in blender lid (to avoid splatters). Blend until smooth. Strain sauce through a fine mesh sieve back into pan; discard solids. Repeat procedure with remaining cooked tomato sauce. Add cheesecloth bag, sugar, and salt to pan, and bring to a boil. Reduce heat, and simmer, uncovered, until reduced to 1 cup (about 45 minutes).

Note: This recipes makes 1 cup of ketchup. To store, let the ketchup cool completely. Transfer it to an airtight container, and store in the refrigerator for up to 3 months.

SERVES 16 (SERVING SIZE: 1 TABLESPOON)
CALORIES 23; FAT 0.2G (SAT 0G, MONO 0.1G, POLY 0.1G); PROTEIN 1G; CARB 5G; FIBER 1G; CHOL 0MG; IRON 0MG; SODIUM 79MG; CALC 11MG

homemade
MAYONNAISE

HANDS-ON TIME: 6 MIN. TOTAL TIME: 6 MIN.

2	teaspoons fresh lemon juice
1	teaspoon Dijon mustard
1	large pasteurized egg yolk
½	cup canola oil
¼	cup olive oil
¼	teaspoon salt
⅛	teaspoon freshly ground black pepper

1. Combine first 3 ingredients in a medium bowl; stir well with a whisk. Combine oils; slowly drizzle oil mixture into egg mixture, stirring constantly with a whisk until mixture is thick and smooth. Stir in salt and pepper.

Note: Store the mayonnaise in an airtight container in the refrigerator for up to 1 week.

SERVES 12 (SERVING SIZE: 1 TABLESPOON)

CALORIES 127; FAT 14.4G (SAT 1.5G, MONO 9G, POLY 3.5G); PROTEIN 0G; CARB 0G; FIBER 0G; CHOL 17MG; IRON 0MG; SODIUM 53MG; CALC 2MG

TARTAR SAUCE

HANDS-ON TIME: 6 MIN. TOTAL TIME: 6 MIN.

You may have only bought tartar sauce in a jar until now. This recipe shows you how easy it is to make your own at home. Pair it with your favorite oven-fried fish or shellfish.

½	cup Homemade Mayonnaise or canola mayonnaise
2	tablespoons sweet pickle relish
2	teaspoons chopped fresh parsley
2	teaspoons minced fresh onion
½	teaspoon fresh lemon juice
½	teaspoon Dijon mustard

1. Combine all ingredients in a small bowl; stir well.

Note: Store the tartar sauce in an airtight container in the refrigerator for up to 1 week.

SERVES 10 (SERVING SIZE: 1 TABLESPOON)

CALORIES 106; FAT 11.5G (SAT 1.2G, MONO 7.2G, POLY 2.8G); PROTEIN 0G; CARB 1G; FIBER 0G; CHOL 14MG; IRON 0MG; SODIUM 70MG; CALC 2MG

TECHNIQUE

Making Mayonnaise

1. The key to creamy home-made mayo is to add a few drops of oil at a time to the egg mixture, then pour in a slow, thin drizzle—whisking constantly—to ensure the mayonnaise blends smoothly.

2. The mixture will thicken as you stir in the oil. Use plain or experiment with added flavorings such as hot sauce or roasted garlic.

STEP 1

STEP 2

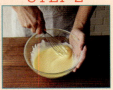

Memphis
BARBECUE SAUCE

HANDS-ON TIME: 10 MIN. TOTAL TIME: 10 MIN.

As the center of Southern barbecue, Memphis offers sauces that occupy the middle ground between different American styles. This blend provides just the right amount of sweet, heat, and tang, which add up to a lot of flavor.

1   cup Heirloom Tomato Ketchup (page 174) or ketchup
¾   cup white vinegar
2   tablespoons brown sugar
2   tablespoons prepared mustard
2   tablespoons Worcestershire sauce
1   tablespoon onion powder
½   teaspoon freshly ground black pepper
¼   teaspoon salt
⅛   teaspoon ground red pepper

1. Combine all ingredients in a medium saucepan; bring to a simmer. Cook 5 minutes, stirring occasionally.

Note: This recipe makes 2 cups. Serve warm. Store in an airtight container in the refrigerator for up to 3 months.

SERVES 16 (SERVING SIZE: 2 TABLESPOONS)
CALORIES 34; FAT 0.3G (SAT 0G, MONO 0.1G, POLY 0.1G); PROTEIN 1G; CARB 8G; FIBER 1G; CHOL 0MG; IRON 0MG; SODIUM 158MG; CALC 18MG

white
BBQ SAUCE

HANDS-ON TIME: 10 MIN. TOTAL TIME: 10 MIN.

This Alabama staple uses mayonnaise as its base instead of tomato sauce, and it's not served hot. Fresh ground pepper is key to this peppery, creamy, and tangy medium-thick sauce—it's meant to be a tad spicy.

1   cup Homemade Mayonnaise (page 176) or canola mayonnaise
¼   cup white vinegar
1   teaspoon freshly ground black pepper
¼   teaspoon salt

1. Combine all ingredients in a medium bowl.

Note: This recipe yields 1 cup. Store in an airtight container in the refrigerator for up to 1 week.

SERVES 16 (SERVING SIZE: 1 TABLESPOON)
CALORIES 100; FAT 11G (SAT 1G, MONO 6G, POLY 3G); PROTEIN 0G; CARB 0G; FIBER 0G; CHOL 5MG; IRON 0MG; SODIUM 136MG; CALC 1MG

MORE IDEAS

Try this sauce with grilled, roasted, or smoked chicken or pork; mixed into shredded cabbage for coleslaw; served over baked potatoes; or used as a spread for chicken or turkey sandwiches.

four-herb

GREEN GODDESS DRESSING

HANDS-ON TIME: 17 MIN. TOTAL TIME: 17 MIN.

Make this creamy green dressing in summer, when herbs are abundant. Both tarragon and chervil (a member of the parsley family) have hints of licorice. If you can't find chervil, use more parsley and tarragon. We replaced some of the mayonnaise with fat-free Greek yogurt for a lighter dressing.

1   cup plain fat-free Greek yogurt
½   cup Homemade Mayonnaise (page 176) or canola mayonnaise
2   teaspoons Worcestershire sauce
2   teaspoons fresh lemon juice
½   teaspoon hot pepper sauce (such as Tabasco)
3   canned anchovy fillets
1   garlic clove, minced
⅔   cup parsley leaves
¼   cup tarragon leaves
¼   cup chopped fresh chives
¼   cup chervil leaves

1. Place first 7 ingredients in a blender or food processor; process until smooth. Add parsley, tarragon, chives, and chervil; process until herbs are minced.

Note: This recipe yield 1½ cups. Store in an airtight container in the refrigerator for up to 3 days.

SERVES 24 (SERVING SIZE: 1 TABLESPOON)
CALORIES 53; FAT 3.2G (SAT 0G, MONO 1.9G, POLY 1.2G); PROTEIN 3G; CARB 2G; FIBER 1G; CHOL 1MG; IRON 1MG; SODIUM 154MG; CALC 63MG

MORE IDEAS

Serve this dressing on a wedge of iceberg lettuce or over butter lettuce, stir it into chicken salad, or offer as a dip for crudités. It's especially good on cucumber wedges and sugar snap peas.

sweet-and-sour bacon
VINAIGRETTE

HANDS-ON TIME: 10 MIN. TOTAL TIME: 10 MIN.

Longing for a warm spinach salad? Make this zippy dressing with bacon, and toss it with red onions, fresh spinach, and a quartered boiled egg. Deglazing the hot pan with vinegar helps scrape up all the tasty browned bits stuck on the bottom.

2   center-cut bacon slices
1½ tablespoons cider vinegar
1½ teaspoons brown sugar
1½ teaspoons Dijon mustard
⅛   teaspoon freshly ground black pepper
Dash of kosher salt

1. Cook bacon until crisp. Remove bacon from pan; crumble. Add vinegar, brown sugar, Dijon mustard, pepper, and salt to drippings in pan, stirring with a whisk. Stir in bacon.

Note: This recipe makes ¼ cup. Store in an airtight container in the refrigerator for up to 2 days. Bring the dressing to room temperature before serving.

SERVES 4 (SERVING SIZE: 1 TABLESPOON)
CALORIES 20; FAT 0.7G (SAT 0.3G, MONO 0.1G, POLY 0.1G); PROTEIN 1G; CARB 2G; FIBER 0G; CHOL 3MG; IRON 0MG; SODIUM 119MG; CALC 2MG

tomato-basil
VINAIGRETTE

HANDS-ON TIME: 6 MIN. TOTAL TIME: 6 MIN.

No need to cut up tomatoes for this simple recipe. Just drop grape tomatoes into your mini food processor. You'll get a zesty salad dressing or a sauce that perks up flank steak or fish. For a change of pace, drizzle it over Homemade Mozzarella (page 120).

2   tablespoons minced fresh basil
2   tablespoons balsamic vinegar
1   tablespoon minced shallots
1   teaspoon Dijon mustard
10   grape tomatoes
1   garlic clove, peeled
2   tablespoons olive oil

1. Place basil, vinegar, shallots, mustard, tomatoes, and garlic clove in a mini food processor, and process until smooth. With processor on, gradually add olive oil, processing until combined.

Note: This recipe yields ½ cup. Store in an airtight container in the refrigerator for up to 3 days. Bring the dressing to room temperature before serving.

SERVES 8 (SERVING SIZE: 1 TABLESPOON)
CALORIES 37; FAT 3.4G (SAT 0.5G, MONO 2.5G, POLY 0.4G); PROTEIN 0G; CARB 1G; FIBER 0G; CHOL 0MG; IRON 0MG; SODIUM 17MG; CALC 4MG

Chapter 6

SNACKS

Sometimes, what you're really craving for a snack is a salty cracker, a crunchy chip and creamy dip, or a chocolaty cookie. This chapter gives you all those options in a healthier form that still satisfies your savory and sweet cravings.

On the salty side, our versions of chips and crackers keep all the flavors and textures you love with less sodium and saturated fat and no artificial trans fats. Good-for-you crispy, crunchy crackers and flatbreads are surprisingly easy to make. The dough comes together quickly, without kneading or yeast. You don't need special equipment, just a rolling pin and a baking sheet.

For your sweet tooth, healthier graham crackers, caramel corn, sandwich cookies, and granola bars contain less sugar and more heart-healthy fats. In addition to these, you'll also find fruit leathers and hot beverage mixes. An added bonus: Some recipes, like the Peanut Butter Caramel Corn (page 211) and the Chai Tea Mix (page 236), make lovely gifts for the holidays.

nacho cheese
TORTILLA CHIPS

◇◇

HANDS-ON TIME: 30 MIN. TOTAL TIME: 2 HR. 15 MIN.

◇◇

If you love Doritos, this is an easy way to make them at home without frying. Using a zip-top plastic bag is the easiest way to get the chips evenly coated with the seasoning mixture, which you can also use in meat fillings for tacos or stir into sour cream to make a cheesy dip.

◇◇

½   cup nacho seasoning
1   teaspoon salt
1   teaspoon sugar
¾   teaspoon onion powder
½   teaspoon garlic powder
½   teaspoon smoked paprika
⅛   teaspoon dry mustard
⅛   teaspoon ground red pepper
40 (6-inch) yellow corn tortillas or Corn
     Tortillas (page 108)
⅓   cup canola oil
Cooking spray

1. Preheat oven to 350°.
2. Combine first 8 ingredients in a bowl. Reserve half of nacho seasoning mixture (about ⅓ cup) in bowl; spoon remaining cheese mixture into an airtight container, and store for another use.
3. Brush both sides of tortillas with oil. Layer 5 tortillas in a stack on a cutting board. Cut stack into 6 wedges, creating 30 triangles. Repeat procedure with remaining tortillas. Arrange 30 triangles on a baking sheet coated with cooking spray (cover remaining wedges to keep from drying).
4. Bake at 350° for 7 minutes; turn chips over, and bake an additional 7 minutes or until edges begin to curl and chips are lightly browned and crisp.
5. Transfer chips to a large heavy-duty zip-top plastic bag. Sprinkle with 2 teaspoons reserved nacho seasoning mixture; seal bag. Shake bag to coat. Transfer chips to a wire rack. Cool completely. Repeat procedure with remaining triangles and remaining reserved nacho seasoning mixture.

Note: Store these chips in an airtight container or zip-top plastic bag at room temperature for up to 3 days. Recrisp them in a 325° oven for 5 minutes, if necessary.

◇◇

SERVES 24 (SERVING SIZE: 10 CHIPS)
CALORIES 125; FAT 4.3G (SAT 0.4G, MONO 2.3G, POLY 1.5G); PROTEIN 2G; CARB 18G; FIBER 3G; CHOL 0MG; IRON 1MG; SODIUM 217MG; CALC 33MG

microwave

SWEET POTATO CHIPS

HANDS-ON TIME: 10 MIN. TOTAL TIME: 30 MIN.

It may sound impossible, but you can create crispy potato chips without deep frying or even baking. The answer is the microwave. Use a mandoline to slice the potato thin enough to crisp, and then just place the slices on parchment paper and zap until crunchy.

Cooking spray
1   (14-ounce) sweet potato, very thinly sliced
1   teaspoon finely chopped fresh rosemary
½   teaspoon salt
¼   teaspoon freshly ground black pepper

1. Cut a circle of parchment paper to fit a microwave-safe plate; coat parchment lightly with cooking spray. Cover plate with parchment paper; arrange one-fourth of the potato slices in a single layer on parchment. Sprinkle evenly with ¼ teaspoon rosemary, ⅛ teaspoon salt, and a dash of pepper. Microwave at power level 9 for 4 minutes. Check for crispness. Continue to cook at 30-second intervals until done. Repeat procedure with remaining potato, rosemary, salt, and pepper.

Note: Store these chips in an airtight container or zip-top plastic bag at room temperature for up to 3 days.

SERVES 8 (SERVING SIZE: 12 CHIPS)

CALORIES 43; FAT 0.1G (SAT 0G, MONO 0.1G, POLY 0G); PROTEIN 1G; CARB 10G; FIBER 2G; CHOL 0MG; IRON 0MG; SODIUM 175MG; CALC 15MG

Crispy Potato Chips

Cut 1 medium purple sweet potato (about 8 ounces) and 1 medium baking potato (about 8 ounces) crosswise into ⅛-inch-thick slices. Combine 1 tablespoon extra-virgin olive oil and ¼ teaspoon salt in a large bowl. Add potatoes; toss gently to coat. Cut a circle of parchment paper to fit a microwave-safe plate. Cover plate with parchment paper; arrange purple potato slices in a single layer over paper. Microwave at HIGH for 4 minutes or until potatoes are crisp and begin to brown. Repeat procedure with baking potatoes, reusing parchment paper.

Note: Store these chips in an airtight container or zip-top plastic bag at room temperature for up to 3 days.

SERVES 8 (SERVING SIZE: ABOUT 13 CHIPS)

CALORIES 59; FAT 1.7G (SAT 0.2G, MONO 1.2G, POLY 0.2G); PROTEIN 1G; CARB 10G; FIBER 1G; CHOL 0MG; IRON 0MG; SODIUM 89MG; CALC 8MG

PITA CHIPS

HANDS-ON TIME: 5 MIN. TOTAL TIME: 11 MIN.

There's nothing like a crispy pita chip, still warm from the oven, to dip in any kind of hummus (page 229) or creamy dip. The combination of salt and crunch with a wallop of creamy dip is especially satisfying.

2   (6-inch) whole-wheat pitas or Whole-Wheat
      Pita Bread (page 105)
Cooking spray
¼   teaspoon salt
¼   teaspoon paprika

1. Preheat oven to 400°.
2. Cut each pita into 16 wedges. Carefully peel apart each wedge to make 2 thinner wedges. Arrange wedges in a single layer on a baking sheet coated with cooking spray. Lightly coat wedges with cooking spray; sprinkle with salt and paprika. Bake at 400° for 6 minutes or until lightly browned and crisp.

Note: Store these chips in an airtight container or zip-top plastic bag at room temperature for up to 1 week.

SERVES 8 (SERVING SIZE: 8 CHIPS)
CALORIES 43; FAT 0.4G (SAT 0.1G, MONO 0.1G, POLY 0.2G); PROTEIN 2G; CARB 9G; FIBER 1G; CHOL 0MG; IRON 1MG; SODIUM 158MG; CALC 3MG

chipotle
TORTILLA CHIPS

◇◇

HANDS-ON TIME: 5 MIN. TOTAL TIME: 27 MIN.

◇◇

Yes, supermarket shelves are bursting with chips, but when you make your own you get chips of uncommon flavor and sturdiness. These are sprinkled with a little chipotle chile powder for zing, but if you or your kids are not up for the spice, feel free to cut back. Dip these chips in Roasted Hatch Chile Salsa (page 225) or Salsa Verde (page 226).

◇◇

8 (6-inch) corn tortillas or Corn Tortillas
    (page 108)
Cooking spray
½ teaspoon salt
½ teaspoon chipotle chile powder

1. Preheat oven to 375°.
2. Cut each tortilla into 8 wedges; arrange tortilla wedges in a single layer on 2 baking sheets coated with cooking spray. Sprinkle wedges with ½ teaspoon salt and chile powder; lightly coat wedges with cooking spray. Bake at 375° for 12 minutes or until wedges are crisp and lightly browned. Cool 10 minutes.

Note: Store these chips in an airtight container or zip-top plastic bag at room temperature for up to 1 week.

◇◇

SERVES 8 (SERVING SIZE: 8 CHIPS)
CALORIES 42; FAT 0.7G (SAT 0G, MONO 0.1G, POLY 0.4G); PROTEIN 1G; CARB 9G; FIBER 1G; CHOL 0MG; IRON 0MG; SODIUM 155MG; CALC 10MG

DAIRY-FREE

NUT-FREE

EGG-FREE

GLUTEN-FREE

PLANTAIN CHIPS

HANDS-ON TIME: 6 MIN. TOTAL TIME: 12 MIN.

Plantains look like large bananas, but they taste bitter when raw. Cooking them brings out their sugars. To bake plantains instead, arrange the slices on a baking sheet and brush with canola oil. Sprinkle the slices with salt, pepper, and garlic powder. Bake at 350° for 30 to 35 minutes, flipping the plantains once. Use plantains that are moderately ripe (mottled-looking) for this recipe.

1   tablespoon olive oil
2   medium plantains, peeled and cut into ¼-inch diagonal slices (about 2 cups)
¼   teaspoon salt
⅛   teaspoon ground red pepper

1. Heat a large nonstick skillet over medium heat. Add oil to pan; swirl to coat. Add plantain slices; cook 3 minutes on each side or until browned. Sprinkle salt and pepper over chips.

Note: Store these chips in an airtight container or zip-top plastic bag at room temperature for up to 3 days.

SERVES 4 (SERVING SIZE: ½ CUP)
CALORIES 190; FAT 3.9G (SAT 0.5G, MONO 2.5G, POLY 0.3G); PROTEIN 2G; CARB 42G; FIBER 1G; CHOL 0MG; IRON 1MG; SODIUM 152MG; CALC 4MG

GRAHAM CRACKERS

HANDS-ON TIME: 16 MIN. TOTAL TIME: 3 HR. 5 MIN.

If you'd like a cinnamon version of these crackers, sprinkle with cinnamon-sugar before baking.

- 6.75 ounces all-purpose flour (about 1½ cups)
- 4.5 ounces whole-wheat pastry flour (about 1 cup)
- ¼ cup granulated sugar
- ¼ cup packed light brown sugar
- 1 teaspoon baking soda
- ½ teaspoon ground cinnamon
- ¼ teaspoon salt
- ½ cup chilled butter, cut into small pieces
- ¼ cup 1% low-fat milk
- 2 tablespoons honey

1. Weigh or lightly spoon flours into dry measuring cups; level with a knife. Place flours and next 5 ingredients (through salt) in a food processor; process 20 seconds. Add butter; pulse until mixture resembles fine meal.
2. Combine milk and honey in a small bowl; stir with a whisk. Drizzle half of milk mixture over mixture in food processor; pulse 3 times. Drizzle remaining milk mixture over mixture in food processor; pulse 7 times or until dough forms a ball. Divide dough in half; shape each half into a 5-inch square. Wrap in plastic wrap and chill at least 2 hours.
3. Preheat oven to 350°.
4. Working with 1 (5-inch) square of dough at a time, roll into a 10-inch square about ⅛ inch thick on a lightly floured surface or between 2 pieces of parchment paper or plastic wrap. Cut square into 8 (5 x 2½–inch) rectangles.

Transfer rectangles to a baking sheet lined with parchment paper using a large thin metal spatula. Score each rectangle lengthwise down the center and crosswise down the center; pierce dough with a fork.
5. Bake at 350° for 12 to 14 minutes or until golden brown. Cool on pans 5 minutes. Transfer to wire racks; cool completely.

Note: Store graham crackers in an airtight container at room temperature for up to 1 week.

SERVES 16 (SERVING SIZE: 1 GRAHAM CRACKER)

CALORIES 159; FAT 6.1G (SAT 3.7G, MONO 1.5G, POLY 0.3G); PROTEIN 2G; CARB 24G; FIBER 1G; CHOL 15MG; IRON 1MG; SODIUM 169MG; CALC 17MG

STEP 1

STEP 2

STEP 3

STEP 4

TECHNIQUE

Forming Graham Crackers

1. Adding the milk mixture in two parts allows it to be evenly distributed without overprocessing the dough. Drizzle the rest of the milk mixture in and pulse just until it comes together and forms a ball. Don't pulse any longer, as you don't want to overwork the dough.

2. Keeping the dough in a square when working with it can be tricky. The key is to rotate the dough 180° every time you roll it.

3. Use a sharp knife to score the dough lengthwise down the center and crosswise across the center, being careful not to cut all the way through the dough.

4. Use a fork to give each cracker its characteristic look and to prevent the dough from puffing up.

honey-wheat BUTTERY CRACKERS

HANDS-ON TIME: 10 MIN. TOTAL TIME: 2 HR. 35 MIN.

Buttery and salty with a slight sweetness, these are the homemade version of the crackers you love. Whole-wheat flour gives them a nutty taste. Make the dough in a food processor, and chill until ready to roll out. Brushing the tops with egg makes the crackers shiny.

4.5 ounces whole-wheat flour (about 1 cup)
4.5 ounces whole-wheat pastry flour (about 1 cup)
1 teaspoon baking soda
1 tablespoon sugar
1 teaspoon salt, divided
1/4 cup cold unsalted butter
2 tablespoons canola oil
1 tablespoon honey
6 tablespoons water
1 large egg
1 tablespoon water

1. Weigh or lightly spoon flours into dry measuring cups; level with a knife. Place flours, baking soda, sugar, and 1/2 teaspoon salt in a food processor; pulse 3 times. Add cold butter, 1 tablespoon at a time, pulsing until coarse crumbs form. Add canola oil and honey; pulse until blended. With processor on, gradually pour 6 tablespoons water through chute, pulsing until dough just comes together. Divide dough in half; shape each half into a flat disc and wrap in plastic wrap. Chill 2 hours or until firm.

2. Preheat oven to 400°.
3. Working with 1 half at a time, roll dough to 1/8-inch thickness. Cut out crackers using a fluted round 1³/₄-inch cutter, rerolling dough once. Pierce each cracker decoratively 9 times with the flat end of a 6-inch skewer. Transfer crackers to a baking sheet lined with parchment paper using a thin spatula. Combine egg and 1 tablespoon water in a small bowl, stirring with a whisk. Brush tops of crackers with egg mixture; sprinkle evenly with 1/2 teaspoon salt.
4. Bake at 400° for 10 minutes or until lightly browned. Transfer to a wire rack; cool completely.

Note: You can store them in an airtight container in your pantry for up to 1 week. The dough can be stored in the refrigerator for up to 1 week or in the freezer for up to 2 months.

SERVES 18 (SERVING SIZE: 4 CRACKERS)

CALORIES 98; FAT 4.6G (SAT 1.9G, MONO 1.4G, POLY 0.9G); PROTEIN 2G; CARB 13G; FIBER 1G; CHOL 17MG; IRON 0MG; SODIUM 206MG; CALC 8MG

cheddar cheese
SNACK CRACKERS

HANDS-ON TIME: 32 MIN. TOTAL TIME: 1 HR. 52 MIN.

Love Cheese Nips? You'll be amazed by how closely our recipe mirrors the original. A sharp cheddar gives these crackers a punch of flavor, while the turmeric and red pepper add natural color and a little bite.

6.75 ounces all-purpose flour (about 1½ cups)
1   cup (4 ounces) shredded reduced-fat sharp cheddar cheese
⅓   cup chilled unsalted butter
1½ teaspoons kosher salt
1   teaspoon baking powder
½   teaspoon ground turmeric
⅛   teaspoon ground red pepper
½   cup water

1. Weigh or lightly spoon flour into dry measuring cups; level with a knife. Place flour and next 6 ingredients (through red pepper) in a food processor; pulse until coarse crumbs form. Add ½ cup water through food chute, 1 tablespoon at a time, pulsing until dough forms a ball. Divide dough in half. Press each half of dough gently into a 4-inch circle on plastic wrap; cover. Chill 1 hour.
2. Preheat oven to 375°.
3. Place half of dough in center between 2 baking sheet–sized pieces of parchment paper; keep other half of dough in refrigerator. Roll dough into a 10-inch square, ⅛ inch thick. Carefully remove top piece of parchment paper. Cut dough into 81 (about 1-inch) squares using a fluted pastry wheel or knife. Pierce a hole in center of each square with a wooden pick. Place squares, ½ inch apart, on 2 parchment paper–lined baking sheets using a wide thin spatula.
4. Bake each pan of squares at 375° for 20 minutes or until crisp. Transfer crackers to wire racks. Cool completely. Repeat procedure with remaining half of dough.

Note: Store the crackers in an airtight container at room temperature for up to 1 week. Recrisp in a 325° oven for 5 minutes, if necessary.

SERVES 27 (SERVING SIZE: 6 CRACKERS)
CALORIES 58; FAT 3.1G (SAT 1.9G, MONO 0.8G, POLY 0.2G); PROTEIN 2G; CARB 6G; FIBER 0G; CHOL 8MG; IRON 0MG; SODIUM 154MG; CALC 52MG

nutty whole-grain
CRACKERS

HANDS-ON TIME: 10 MIN. TOTAL TIME: 1 HR. 35 MIN.

These crunchy, nutty crackers are as good with a little peanut butter as they would be with a slice of cheddar or Brie. Three kinds of seeds are ground right into the dough, along with whole-wheat flour and almond meal. If cutting out the crackers with a cookie cutter, don't gather the scraps and reroll the dough to get additional crackers—they'll end up tough. Instead, just bake the scraps as they are.

4.75 ounces whole-wheat flour (about 1 cup)
¼ **cup almond meal**
¼ **cup pumpkinseed kernels**
2 **tablespoons flaxseed meal**
2 **tablespoons sunflower seed kernels**
1 **teaspoon caraway seeds**
1 **teaspoon onion powder**
¾ **teaspoon salt**
½ **teaspoon garlic powder**
2 **tablespoons butter, cut into pieces**
2 **tablespoons olive oil**
3 **tablespoons water**
1 **large egg, lightly beaten**

1. Preheat oven to 275°.
2. Weigh or lightly spoon flour into a dry measuring cup; level with a knife. Place flour and next 8 ingredients (through garlic powder) in a food processor; process until seeds are almost completely ground. Add butter and remaining ingredients; process until dough pulls away from sides of processor bowl.
3. Cut 2 (12-inch) squares of parchment paper. Place 1 square of parchment paper on a large baking sheet; place dough in center. Press dough with fingers to form a square. Place second square of parchment paper on top of dough; roll dough into a 10-inch square, about ⅛ inch thick.
4. Remove top piece of parchment paper. Cut dough into 25 (2-inch) squares. Separate squares slightly (do not remove from parchment paper). Freeze 5 minutes.
5. Bake at 275° for 1 hour and 5 minutes or until crisp. Cool completely on wire racks.

Note: Store the crackers in an airtight container at room temperature for up to 1 week.

SERVES 25 (SERVING SIZE: 1 CRACKER)
CALORIES 60; FAT 4G (SAT 1G, MONO 1.4G, POLY 0.7G); PROTEIN 2G; CARB 5G; FIBER 1G; CHOL 10MG; IRON 0MG; SODIUM 83MG; CALC 9MG

STEP 1 · STEP 2

◊◊◊ TECHNIQUE ◊◊◊
How to Cut the Crackers

1. A sharp knife will certainly work to cut the crackers into squares, but a pizza cutter makes easy work of it, too.

2. You could also cut the dough into diamonds or use cookie cutters to create whatever shapes you wish.

Parmesan-rosemary
FLATBREAD CRACKERS

HANDS-ON TIME: 1 HR. 20 MIN. TOTAL TIME: 1 HR. 20 MIN.

Crisp and buttery, these cheesy flatbread crackers with a hint of rosemary make an indulgent snack or an upscale cracker for entertaining. The dough is kneaded gently, and then portioned and rolled out right on parchment paper, which goes onto a preheated baking sheet. No cutting required.

6.75 ounces all-purpose flour (about 1½ cups)
3 tablespoons finely ground flaxseed meal
1½ tablespoons chopped fresh rosemary
1 teaspoon baking powder
¼ teaspoon freshly ground black pepper
1.5 ounces Parmigiano-Reggiano cheese, grated (about ⅓ cup)
½ cup water
⅓ cup butter, softened
1½ teaspoons kosher salt

1. Place a baking sheet on the middle rack in oven. Preheat oven to 425° (keep pan in oven as it preheats).
2. Weigh or lightly spoon flour into dry measuring cups; level with a knife. Combine flour and next 5 ingredients (through cheese) in a large bowl. Make a well in center of mixture; add ½ cup water and butter. Stir with a wooden spoon until dough pulls together in a shaggy mass. Turn dough out onto a lightly floured work surface; knead gently 6 to 8 times or until dough is smooth and soft.
3. Divide dough into 8 equal portions. Working with 1 portion at a time (keep remaining portions covered with a damp towel to prevent drying), divide into 3 equal pieces. Place 3 dough pieces 3 inches apart in the center of a baking sheet–sized piece of parchment paper. Top with another piece of parchment paper. Roll dough pieces into long oval shapes, about 6 x 3 inches (dough will be very thin). Carefully remove top piece of parchment. Sprinkle each dough section with ¹⁄₁₆ teaspoon salt, pressing to adhere.
4. Place parchment with rolled dough on preheated baking sheet. Bake at 425° for 5 minutes or until crackers are browned in spots. Remove parchment and crackers from oven, and place on a wire rack to cool. Repeat procedure with the remaining dough and salt.

Note: These crackers can be stored in an airtight container at room temperature for up to 3 days.

SERVES 24 (SERVING SIZE: 1 CRACKER)
CALORIES 60; FAT 3.2G (SAT 1.8G, MONO 0.8G, POLY 0.4G); PROTEIN 2G; CARB 6G; FIBER 1G; CHOL 8MG; IRON 1MG; SODIUM 180MG; CALC 27MG

lemon-Parmesan
POPCORN

HANDS-ON TIME: 8 MIN. TOTAL TIME: 9 MIN.

Lemon and Parmesan is a classic Italian combination for salads, fish, soup, and vegetables. It's also delectable on popcorn. To make sure the oil is hot enough for the popcorn, add a couple of kernels and wait for them to pop. Once they pop, add the remaining kernels.

2   teaspoons grated lemon rind
1   teaspoon freshly ground black pepper
¼   teaspoon kosher salt
1.5 ounces Parmigiano-Reggiano cheese, finely
     grated (about ⅓ cup)
2   tablespoons olive oil
½   cup unpopped popcorn kernels

1. Combine lemon rind, pepper, salt, and Parmigiano-Reggiano cheese in a small bowl.
2. Heat a medium, heavy saucepan over medium-high heat. Add oil to pan; swirl to coat. Add popcorn to oil in pan; cover and cook 2 minutes or until kernels begin to pop, shaking pan frequently. Continue cooking 1 minute, shaking pan constantly. When popping slows down, remove pan from heat. Let stand 1 minute or until all popping stops.
3. Pour 6 cups popcorn into a large bowl; stir in half of cheese mixture. Stir in remaining 6 cups popcorn and remaining half of cheese mixture; toss to coat. Let stand 1 minute before serving.

Note: Store in an airtight container at room temperature for up to 3 days.

SERVES 6 (SERVING SIZE: 2 CUPS)
CALORIES 128; FAT 7.2G (SAT 1.9G, MONO 3.9G, POLY 0.6G); PROTEIN 4G; CARB 12G; FIBER 3G; CHOL 6MG; IRON 1MG; SODIUM 189MG; CALC 81MG

peanut butter
CARAMEL CORN

HANDS-ON TIME: 14 MIN. TOTAL TIME: 1 HR. 30 MIN.

Here's a snack for those times when you want salt, sugar, fat, and crunch all in one bite. There's just enough butter to create a layer of caramel goodness. Peanut butter and sliced almonds provide richness. Make it for yourself or package for gifts.

Cooking spray
2   tablespoons canola oil
½   cup unpopped popcorn kernels
½   cup sliced almonds
⅔   cup packed brown sugar
⅔   cup light-colored corn syrup
2½ tablespoons butter
½   teaspoon salt
½   cup Peanut Butter (page 160) or
      natural creamy peanut butter
1   teaspoon vanilla extract

1. Preheat oven to 250°.
2. Line a jelly-roll pan with parchment paper; coat paper with cooking spray.
3. Heat a large Dutch oven over medium-high heat. Add oil to pan; swirl to coat. Add popcorn; cover and cook 4 minutes, shaking pan frequently. When popping slows, remove pan from heat. Let stand until popping stops. Uncover; add almonds.
4. Combine sugar, syrup, butter, and salt in a medium saucepan; bring to a boil. Cook 3 minutes, stirring occasionally. Remove from heat. Add peanut butter and vanilla; stir until smooth. Drizzle over popcorn; toss well. Spread mixture out onto prepared pan. Bake at 250° for 1 hour, stirring every 15 minutes. Cool completely.

Note: Store in an airtight container at room temperature for up to 1 week.

SERVES 20 (SERVING SIZE: ABOUT ¾ CUP)
CALORIES 155; FAT 7.4G (SAT 1.8G, MONO 3.5G, POLY 1.6G); PROTEIN 3G; CARB 21G; FIBER 1G; CHOL 4MG; IRON 0MG; SODIUM 108MG; CALC 17MG

chocolate
MARSHMALLOWS

HANDS-ON TIME: 50 MIN. TOTAL TIME: 2 HR. 50 MIN.

1 cup water, divided
3 (1/4-ounce) packages unflavored gelatin
1 1/2 cups granulated sugar
1 cup light-colored corn syrup
Dash of salt
1 teaspoon vanilla extract
1/4 cup sifted unsweetened cocoa
Cooking spray
1/3 cup powdered sugar
1/3 cup cornstarch
2 teaspoons unsweetened cocoa
2 ounces bittersweet chocolate, chopped

1. Pour 1/2 cup water into a small microwave-safe bowl, and sprinkle with gelatin.
2. Combine 1/2 cup water, granulated sugar, corn syrup, and salt in a medium, heavy saucepan over medium-high heat; bring to a boil, stirring occasionally. Cook, without stirring, until a candy thermometer registers 250°. Pour sugar mixture into the bowl of a stand mixer; let stand until a candy thermometer registers 210°.
3. Microwave gelatin mixture at HIGH 20 seconds or until gelatin melts, stirring after 10 seconds. With mixer on low speed, beat sugar mixture using a whip attachment; gradually pour gelatin mixture in a thin stream into sugar mixture. Add vanilla. Increase speed to high, and whip mixture at high speed until light and fluffy (about 5 minutes). Reduce mixer to medium speed, and gradually add 1/4 cup cocoa; beat until combined. Using a spatula coated with cooking spray, scrape mixture into an 11 x 7–inch baking pan coated with cooking spray; smooth top. Let stand 2 hours.
4. Sift together powdered sugar, cornstarch, and 2 teaspoons cocoa into a jelly-roll pan. Using an offset spatula coated with cooking spray, remove marshmallow from baking pan; place in powdered sugar mixture. Using scissors well coated with powdered sugar mixture, cut marshmallows into 77 (1-inch) squares. Dust with powdered sugar mixture; shake to remove excess sugar mixture.
5. Arrange marshmallows on a cooling rack placed on a jelly-roll pan. Place bittersweet chocolate in a small microwave-safe bowl; microwave at HIGH 1 minute or until melted, stirring every 20 seconds until smooth. Drizzle melted chocolate over marshmallows; let stand until chocolate is set.

Note: Store the marshmallows in an airtight container at room temperature for up to 2 weeks.

SERVES 77 (SERVING SIZE: 1 MARSHMALLOW)
CALORIES 37; FAT 0.4G (SAT 0.2G, MONO 0G, POLY 0G); PROTEIN 0G; CARB 9G; FIBER 0G; CHOL 0MG; IRON 0MG; SODIUM 5MG; CALC 1MG

chocolate crème-filled
SANDWICH COOKIES

◇◇

HANDS-ON TIME: 25 MIN. TOTAL TIME: 3 HR. 11 MIN.

◇◇

Try this recipe and you may never buy Oreos again. This unconventional mixing method makes for an exceptional shortbread-like cookie. If the dough is too soft to shape into a log, chill it for 1 hour.

◇◇

VARIATIONS

Add cocoa powder or mini chocolate chips to the filling for an intensely all-chocolate cookie.

Substitute caramel sauce or peanut butter for the filling.

Cookies:

7.9 ounces all-purpose flour (about 1¾ cups)
¾ cup granulated sugar
⅔ cup unsweetened dark cocoa powder
½ teaspoon baking soda
¼ teaspoon salt
¾ cup butter, cut into small pieces
1 large egg white
1 tablespoon water

Filling:

⅓ cup vegan shortening (such as Earth Balance)
⅓ cup butter, softened
1⅔ cups powdered sugar
1 teaspoon vanilla extract

1. To prepare cookies, weigh or lightly spoon flour into dry measuring cups; level with a knife. Add flour and next 5 ingredients (through butter) to the bowl of a stand mixer. Beat at low speed until crumbly. Add egg white and water; beat until blended.
2. Divide dough in half. Roll each half of dough into an 8½ x 1½–inch log. Wrap in plastic wrap; chill 2 hours.
3. Preheat oven to 350°.
4. Cut each log into 48 (⅛-inch-thick) slices. Place on baking sheets lined with parchment paper.
5. Bake at 350° for 10 to 12 minutes or until set. Cool on pans 2 minutes; transfer cookies to wire racks, and cool completely.
6. To prepare filling, beat shortening and ⅓ cup butter with a mixer at medium speed until smooth. Gradually add powdered sugar, beating at low speed until blended. Beat in vanilla.
7. Spread about 1½ teaspoons filling onto flat side of each of 48 cookies; top with remaining 48 cookies, flat sides down.

Note: You can freeze wrapped logs of dough for up to 1 month. Freeze prepared sandwich cookies in a heavy-duty zip-top plastic bag for up to 3 months. The cookies will keep in an airtight container at room temperature for up to 1 week.

◇◇◇◇◇◇◇◇◇◇◇◇◇◇◇◇◇◇◇◇◇◇◇◇◇◇◇◇◇◇◇

SERVES 48 (SERVING SIZE: 1 COOKIE)

CALORIES 86; FAT 4.5G (SAT 2.8G, MONO 1.2G, POLY 0.2G); PROTEIN 1G; CARB 12G; FIBER 1G; CHOL 11MG; IRON 0MG; SODIUM 64MG; CALC 4MG

peanut butter
SANDWICH COOKIES

HANDS-ON TIME: 20 MIN. TOTAL TIME: 1 HR. 12 MIN.

11.25 ounces all-purpose flour (about 2½ cups)
½ teaspoon baking soda
½ teaspoon baking powder
⅝ teaspoon salt, divided
¾ cup packed brown sugar
1 cup Peanut Butter (page 160) or natural creamy peanut butter, divided
½ cup granulated sugar
¼ cup butter, softened
2 large eggs
2 teaspoons vanilla extract, divided
⅓ cup butter, softened
1½ cups powdered sugar

1. Preheat oven to 350°.
2. Weigh or lightly spoon flour into dry measuring cups; level with a knife. Combine flour, baking soda, baking powder, and ½ teaspoon salt in a medium bowl; stir with a whisk.
3. Beat brown sugar, ½ cup peanut butter, granulated sugar, and ¼ cup softened butter with a mixer at medium speed until light and fluffy. Add eggs, 1 at a time, beating well after each addition. Beat in 1 teaspoon vanilla. Gradually add flour mixture; beat at low speed until well blended. Divide dough in half. Press half of dough into a (6 x 4–inch) rectangle; wrap in plastic wrap and refrigerate.
4. Roll remaining half of dough into a 15 x 9–inch rectangle (⅛ inch thick) on a lightly floured surface. Cut into 36 (2½ x 1½–inch) rectangles. Place rectangles on baking sheets lined with parchment paper.
5. Bake at 350° for 8 to 10 minutes or until edges are golden brown. Cool on pans 2 minutes. Transfer to wire racks; cool completely. Repeat procedure with chilled half of dough.
6. Place ½ cup Peanut Butter, ⅓ cup softened butter, and ⅛ teaspoon salt in a medium bowl; beat at medium speed with a mixer until smooth. Gradually add powdered sugar, beating at low speed until blended. Beat in 1 teaspoon vanilla.
7. Spread about 2 teaspoons filling onto flat side of each of 36 cookies; top with remaining 36 cookies, flat side down.

Note: You can freeze wrapped rectangles of dough for up to 1 month. The prepared sandwich cookies will keep in the freezer in a heavy-duty zip-top plastic bag for up to 3 months. The cookies will keep in an airtight container at room temperature for up to 1 week.

SERVES 36 (SERVING SIZE: 1 SANDWICH COOKIE)
CALORIES 155; FAT 6.9G (SAT 2.4G, MONO 2.3G, POLY 0.9G); PROTEIN 3G; CARB 21G; FIBER 1G; CHOL 18MG; IRON 1MG; SODIUM 123MG; CALC 12MG

no-bake PB–chocolate chip
GRANOLA SQUARES

HANDS-ON TIME: 6 MIN. TOTAL TIME: 1 HR. 6 MIN.

Substitute your favorite nut butter, such as almond or cashew butter, for the peanut butter. If you'd like to avoid gluten, substitute flaxseed for the wheat germ. If you don't have walnuts on hand, chopped almonds are a good substitute.

Cooking spray
2   cups old-fashioned rolled oats
1   cup oven-toasted rice cereal
¼   cup toasted wheat germ
¼   cup finely chopped walnuts
⅔   cup Peanut Butter (page 160) or natural creamy peanut butter
½   cup honey
1   teaspoon vanilla extract
⅓   cup semisweet chocolate minichips

1. Line an 8-inch square baking dish with foil that extends 1 inch beyond sides; coat foil with cooking spray.
2. Combine oats and next 3 ingredients (through walnuts) in a large bowl. Combine peanut butter, honey, and vanilla in a 2-cup glass measure. Microwave at HIGH 1 minute or until melted and smooth, stirring after 30 seconds. Pour peanut butter mixture over oat mixture, stirring until oat mixture is coated. Stir in chocolate minichips. Press mixture into prepared dish; chill 1 hour. Remove from pan by lifting foil. Remove foil; cut into 16 squares.

Note: The granola bars will keep in an airtight container at room temperature for up to 1 week.

SERVES 16 (SERVING SIZE: 1 SQUARE)
CALORIES 176; FAT 8.7G (SAT 2G, MONO 3.6G, POLY 2.6G); PROTEIN 5G; CARB 22G; FIBER 2G; CHOL 0MG; IRON 2G; SODIUM 63MG; CALC 8MG

OATMEAL-RAISIN BARS

HANDS-ON: 5 MIN. TOTAL: 2 HR. 10 MIN.

1   cup golden raisins
1   cup boiling water
Cooking spray
1   cup quick-cooking oats
1   cup walnuts
½   teaspoon vanilla extract
¼   teaspoon fine sea salt
¼   teaspoon ground cinnamon

1. Combine raisins and boiling water in a bowl; cover and let stand 5 minutes or until soft. Drain and pat dry with paper towels.
2. Line a 9 x 5–inch loaf pan with plastic wrap. Coat plastic wrap with cooking spray. Place oats in a food processor; process 30 seconds or until finely ground. Add raisins, walnuts, and remaining ingredients; process 1 minute or until mixture is finely chopped and pulls away from sides of processor bowl.
3. Transfer fruit mixture to prepared pan. Coat a piece of plastic wrap with cooking spray. Place plastic wrap, sprayed side down, on surface, and press into an even layer using your fingers. Leave plastic wrap pressed directly onto fruit mixture to cover; chill 2 hours.
4. Cut fruit mixture into 6 bars. Wrap each bar individually with plastic wrap.

Note: Store in the refrigerator up to 2 weeks.

SERVES 6 (SERVING SIZE: 1 BAR)
CALORIES 252; FAT 12.4G (SAT 1.1G, MONO 1.8G, POLY 7.9G); PROTEIN 5G; CARB 34G; FIBER 4G; CHOL 0MG; IRON 2MG; SODIUM 97MG; CALC 41MG

Cherry Pie Bars

Combine 1 cup boiling water, ⅓ cup whole pitted dates, and 1 (5-ounce) package dried tart cherries in a bowl; cover and let stand 10 minutes or until soft. Drain and pat dry with paper towels. Place cherry mixture, 1 cup raw unblanched almonds, ½ teaspoon vanilla extract, and ¼ teaspoon fine sea salt in a food processor; process 1 minute or until mixture is finely chopped and pulls away from sides of processor bowl. Transfer fruit mixture to prepared pan and prepare as directed.

SERVES 6 (SERVING SIZE: 1 BAR)
CALORIES 244; FAT 13.1G (SAT 1G); SODIUM 101MG

Chocolate–Pecan Pie Bars

Combine 1 cup whole pitted dates and 1 cup boiling water in a bowl; cover and let stand 10 minutes or until soft. Drain and pat dry with paper towels. Place date mixture, 1 cup pecans, ⅓ cup raw unblanched almonds, 2 tablespoons unsweetened cocoa, ½ teaspoon vanilla extract, ¼ teaspoon fine sea salt, and 1 ounce coarsely chopped bittersweet chocolate in a food processor; process 1 minute or until mixture is finely chopped and pulls away from sides of processor, scraping sides of bowl as needed. Transfer fruit mixture to prepared pan and prepare as directed.

SERVES 6 (SERVING SIZE: 1 BAR)
CALORIES 278; FAT 18.6G (SAT 2.7G); SODIUM 96MG

peach-strawberry
FRUIT LEATHER

HANDS-ON TIME: 31 MIN. TOTAL TIME: 7 HR. 1 MIN.

Fruit snacks are sure to be a child's lunchbox favorite. Our version, which has less sugar than the store-bought variety, starts with a puree of fresh fruit that bakes at a low temperature for several hours in a jelly-roll pan. When dry, it's cut and rolled into strips.

2   cups coarsely chopped fresh strawberries
1   cup sliced peeled fresh peaches (2 small)
½   cup water
2   tablespoons honey
1   teaspoon fresh lemon juice

1. Preheat oven to 170°.
2. Line a 15 x 10–inch jelly-roll pan with heavy-duty plastic wrap, allowing plastic wrap to extend over edges of pan.
3. Combine all ingredients in a medium saucepan. Bring to a boil; reduce heat, and simmer 10 minutes or until fruit is tender. Remove from heat; cool 5 minutes.
4. Place fruit mixture in a food processor or blender; process until smooth. Strain fruit puree through a sieve over a bowl; discard solids. Pour strained fruit mixture onto prepared pan, spreading ¼ inch thick to edges of pan with a spatula.
5. Bake at 170° for 6 to 7 hours or until center is just slightly sticky, brushing edges with water after 3 hours if necessary to prevent over-drying. Remove from pan; peel off plastic wrap. Trim excessively dry edges ¼ inch from all sides of leather, if necessary. Cut leather in half lengthwise. Cut each half crosswise into 13 strips (about 1 inch wide). Beginning at 1 end, roll up strips in parchment paper or plastic wrap.

Note: You can store the fruit leathers in an airtight container at room temperature for up to 2 weeks or freeze for 1 month.

SERVES 26 (SERVING SIZE: 1 FRUIT LEATHER STRIP)
CALORIES 11; FAT 0G; PROTEIN 0G; CARB 3G; FIBER 0G; CHOL 0MG; IRON 0MG; SODIUM 0MG; CALC 3MG

STEP 1

STEP 2

TECHNIQUE

Making Fruit Leather

1. It's crucial to spread the mixture to a ¼-inch thickness, and no less. We found that when the mixture was spread thinner, the fruit leather was too brittle and dry. The edges will still get a little dry, but you can simply trim those off.

2. To keep the leather from sticking, roll it up in parchment paper or plastic wrap for easy storage.

DAIRY-FREE

NUT-FREE

EGG-FREE

GLUTEN-FREE

roasted Hatch chile
SALSA

HANDS-ON TIME: 11 MIN. TOTAL TIME: 36 MIN.

Hatch chiles are long, pointed green chiles from New Mexico that can also be red, yellow, orange, or brown when ripe. They're only available in August and September, so if you're a salsa fiend, buy lots, and then roast and freeze them so you can use them throughout the year. They are said to get hotter as they age, so stick with green if you want mildness. The char from broiled vegetables adds smokiness to this simple salsa.

3   Hatch chiles
1   pound tomatoes
4   medium shallots, peeled
3   unpeeled garlic cloves
2   tablespoons chopped fresh cilantro
2½ tablespoons fresh lime juice
¾   teaspoon kosher salt

1. Preheat broiler to high. Place chiles, tomatoes, shallots, and garlic cloves on a baking sheet. Broil vegetable mixture 10 minutes or until charred, turning once after 5 minutes.
2. Remove chiles from pan. Place in a paper bag; fold to close tightly. Let stand 15 minutes. Remove skins, tops, and seeds from chiles; discard. Remove skins from garlic; discard.
3. Place chiles, garlic, tomatoes, shallots, cilantro, lime juice, and kosher salt in the bowl of a food processor; pulse 10 times or until mixture is well combined.

Note: Store the salsa in an airtight container in the refrigerator for up to 1 week.

SERVES 12 (SERVING SIZE: ¼ CUP)
CALORIES 34; FAT 0.2G (SAT 0G, MONO 0G, POLY 0.1G); PROTEIN 2G; CARB 8G; FIBER 1G; CHOL 0MG; IRON 1MG; SODIUM 185MG; CALC 13MG

SALSA VERDE

HANDS-ON TIME: 12 MIN. TOTAL TIME: 44 MIN.

Poblanos are a popular green chile pepper from Mexico. They're usually mild, but occasionally you'll get a hot one. Serranos, the most common chile in Mexican cuisine, are smaller and can be bright red or green, with a bright, biting flavor. Broiling chile peppers delivers a tangible smokiness.

MORE IDEAS

Make a double batch of this salsa verde so you can use it as a dip for Chipotle Tortilla Chips (page 194), and as a fabulous marinade or topping for roasted, stewed, or barbecued chicken or pork.

2   poblano peppers
½   cup unsalted chicken stock or Chicken Stock (page 240)
1   pound tomatillos, peeled
2   tablespoons fresh lime juice
2   garlic cloves, peeled
⅔   cup chopped white onion
⅓   cup chopped cilantro
½   teaspoon kosher salt
1   fresh serrano chile, finely chopped

1. Preheat broiler.
2. Broil poblano peppers 5 minutes per side or until blackened. Place in a small paper bag; seal. Let stand 10 minutes; peel and chop.
3. While peppers broil, bring chicken stock and tomatillos to a boil in a saucepan over medium heat. Cover and simmer 8 minutes.
4. Remove from heat; let stand 20 minutes. Pour into a blender. Add lime juice and garlic cloves; process until smooth. Pour into a bowl; stir in poblanos, onion, cilantro, kosher salt, and chopped serrano chile. Chill.

Note: Store the salsa in an airtight container in the refrigerator for up to 1 week.

SERVES 8 (SERVING SIZE: ¼ CUP)
CALORIES 34; FAT 0.7G (SAT 0.1G, MONO 0.1G, POLY 0.3G); PROTEIN 1G; CARB 7G; FIBER 2G; CHOL 0MG; IRON 0MG; SODIUM 146MG; CALC 10MG

traditional
HUMMUS

HANDS-ON TIME: 5 MIN. TOTAL TIME: 5 MIN.

This Middle Eastern dip lends itself to endless variations. In addition to the options shown here, stir in sun-dried tomatoes and basil or chopped olives. Prepare and refrigerate hummus a day ahead, and let it stand at room temperature for 30 minutes before serving with homemade Pita Chips (page 192).

2   (15.5-ounce) cans no-salt-added chickpeas (garbanzo beans), rinsed and drained
2   garlic cloves, crushed
1/2   cup water
1/4   cup tahini (sesame seed paste)
3   tablespoons fresh lemon juice
2   tablespoons extra-virgin olive oil
3/4   teaspoon salt
1/4   teaspoon freshly ground black pepper

1. Place beans and garlic in a food processor; pulse 5 times or until chopped. Add 1/2 cup water and remaining ingredients; pulse until smooth, scraping down sides as needed.

Note: Store hummus in an airtight container in the refrigerator for up to 5 days.

SERVES 26 (SERVING SIZE: 2 TABLESPOONS)
CALORIES 44; FAT 2.5G (SAT 0.3G, MONO 1.2G, POLY 0.7G); PROTEIN 2G; CARB 4G; FIBER 1G; CHOL 0MG; IRON 0MG; SODIUM 74MG; CALC 12MG

Feta-Baked Hummus

Combine Traditional Hummus, 1/2 cup (2 ounces) crumbled reduced-fat feta cheese, 1/4 cup chopped fresh parsley, and 1/2 teaspoon ground cumin. Transfer mixture to an 8-inch square baking dish coated with cooking spray. Sprinkle with 1/2 cup (2 ounces) crumbled reduced-fat feta cheese. Bake at 400° for 25 minutes or until lightly browned. Garnish with parsley sprigs.

SERVES 32 (SERVING SIZE: 2 TABLESPOONS)
CALORIES 44; FAT 2.5G (SAT 0.6G); SODIUM 109MG

Spicy Red Pepper Hummus

Cut 2 red bell peppers in half lengthwise; discard seeds and membranes. Place pepper halves, skin sides up, on a foil-lined baking sheet; flatten with hand. Broil 15 minutes or until blackened. Place in a zip-top plastic bag; seal. Let stand 10 minutes. Peel and cut into strips. Place bell peppers, 2 teaspoons chile paste with garlic (such as sambal oelek), 1/2 teaspoon paprika, and 1/8 teaspoon ground red pepper in a food processor; pulse until smooth. Transfer pepper mixture to a serving bowl; stir in Traditional Hummus.

SERVES 32 (SERVING SIZE: 2 TABLESPOONS)
CALORIES 39; FAT 2G (SAT 0.3G); SODIUM 74MG

creamy
RANCH-STYLE DIP

HANDS-ON TIME: 7 MIN. TOTAL TIME: 7 MIN.

Make a double batch of this healthier Ranch-style dip, and store leftovers in a jam jar or other airtight container. Serve with baby carrots, broccoli florets, and red pepper spears. You might also spoon it into a Mason jar for a gift, with accompanying homemade crackers or chips.

4   ounces ⅓-less-fat cream cheese, softened
3   tablespoons nonfat buttermilk
2   tablespoons chopped fresh flat-leaf parsley
1   teaspoon chopped fresh dill
½   teaspoon minced fresh garlic
¼   teaspoon onion powder
¼   teaspoon salt
¼   teaspoon freshly ground black pepper
Chopped dill sprigs (optional)

1. Combine cream cheese and buttermilk in a small bowl, stirring with a whisk until blended. Stir in remaining ingredients. Garnish with dill sprigs, if desired.

Note: Store in an airtight container in the refrigerator for up to 10 days.

SERVES 6 (SERVING SIZE: ABOUT 2 TABLESPOONS)

CALORIES 52; FAT 4.3G (SAT 2.4G, MONO 1.1G, POLY 0.2G); PROTEIN 2G; CARB 1G; FIBER 0G; CHOL 14MG; IRON 0MG; SODIUM 170MG; CALC 34MG

sour cream and onion
DIP

HANDS-ON TIME: 18 MIN. TOTAL TIME: 18 MIN.

Remember the dried onion dip you stirred into sour cream? Make this healthier version with fresh ingredients instead. Cooking the onions and garlic reduces their harshness and caramelizes them for a sweeter taste. Chives add additional onion flavor and color. Serve with cherry tomatoes, bell peppers slices, batons of carrots and celery, or Microwave Sweet Potato Chips (page 191), Crispy Potato Chips (page 191), or Pita Chips (page 192).

1 teaspoon canola oil
2 cups finely chopped sweet yellow onion (about 1 onion)
1 tablespoon minced fresh garlic
¼ teaspoon salt, divided
1 cup reduced-fat sour cream
½ cup canola mayonnaise or Homemade Mayonnaise (page 176)
2 tablespoons minced fresh chives, divided
¼ teaspoon ground white pepper

1. Heat a small skillet over medium-high heat. Add oil to pan; swirl to coat. Add onion, garlic, and ⅛ teaspoon salt; cook 4 minutes, stirring frequently. Reduce heat to medium-low; cook 6 minutes, stirring frequently. Cool onion mixture slightly.

2. Combine sour cream, mayonnaise, 1½ tablespoons chives, pepper, and ⅛ teaspoon salt in a large bowl. Add onion mixture; stir well. Top with 1½ teaspoons chives.

Note: Store in an airtight container in the refrigerator for up to 2 weeks.

SERVES 12 (SERVING SIZE: ABOUT 2 TABLESPOONS)

CALORIES 67; FAT 5.3G (SAT 1.5G, MONO 2.5G, POLY 1.1G); PROTEIN 1G; CARB 4G; FIBER 1G; CHOL 8MG; IRON 0MG; SODIUM 139MG; CALC 29MG

spiced
MOCHA MIX

◇◇◇

HANDS-ON TIME: 5 MIN. TOTAL TIME: 5 MIN.

◇◇◇

For those nights when a cup of something chocolaty is exactly what you need, here's a healthier cocoa mix with hints of cinnamon and nutmeg to warm you.

◇◇◇

2 cups unsweetened cocoa
1¾ cups sugar
¼ cup instant espresso powder
2 teaspoons ground cinnamon
1 teaspoon freshly grated nutmeg

1. Combine all ingredients in a large bowl; stir well. Store in an airtight container. To prepare each serving, stir 1½ tablespoons mix into 8 ounces hot milk.

Note: This recipe makes 3½ cups. Store the mix in an airtight container in the pantry for up to 6 months. Shake well before each use.

◇◇

SERVES 37 (SERVING SIZE: 1½ TABLESPOONS)

CALORIES 47; FAT 0.5G (SAT 0G, MONO 0.2G, POLY 0.1G); PROTEIN 1G; CARB 12G; FIBER 2G; CHOL 0MG; IRON 0MG; SODIUM 0MG; CALC 2MG

chai TEA MIX

HANDS-ON TIME: 5 MIN. TOTAL TIME: 5 MIN.

Give an instant boost to a cup of hot black tea on a gray day with this easy mix. Make more for holiday gifts and package in Mason jars, or spoon some into a clear cello bag and stuff into an oversized mug.

1 cup nonfat dry milk
½ cup sugar
½ teaspoon ground ginger
½ teaspoon ground cardamom
½ teaspoon ground cinnamon
¼ teaspoon ground allspice
⅛ teaspoon ground nutmeg
⅛ teaspoon ground cloves
Dash of ground red pepper

1. Combine all ingredients. To prepare each serving, stir 1½ tablespoons tea mix into 8 ounces hot brewed black tea.

Note: Store in an airtight container in the pantry for up to 6 months.

SERVES 16 (SERVING SIZE: 1½ TABLESPOONS)
CALORIES 40; FAT 0G; PROTEIN 2G; CARB 9G; FIBER 0G; CHOL 1MG; IRON 0MG; SODIUM 24MG; CALC 54MG

VARIATIONS

You can use this recipe as a base to play around with spices to find other combinations you enjoy. If you have vanilla sugar on hand, substitute it for regular sugar. If you like heat, ground white pepper adds a slightly different kick than red. For an intense scent, try adding ground dried orange peel.

Chapter 7

STOCKS & SAUCES

Making your own stocks and sauces leads to weeknight meals full of flavor and variety. When your pantry includes these items, you have choices: Use Chicken or Simple Vegetable Stock (page 240) as the base for a quick soup, spoon Cheddar Cheese Sauce (page 255) over steamed broccoli or cauliflower, serve Quick Gravy (page 246) with roast chicken, or rich Béchamel Sauce (page 249) over pasta. A few cold sauces, like Ponzu (page 260) and Spicy Peanut Dipping Sauce (page 262), perk up Asian noodles and make vegetables, meats, and tofu irresistible.

While these recipes are healthier versions of many classic sauces, they still use smart amounts of ingredients like butter, egg yolks, and whole milk to add richness and flavor. You'll use less sharp cheddar cheese, for example, because of its assertive flavor, while a lower-fat cream cheese rounds out the texture of Quick Gravy.

One stock or sauce leads to many dishes, and we've suggested some here, like Butternut-Kale Lasagna (page 251) made with Mornay Sauce and Crab Eggs Benedict (page 252) made with Mock Hollandaise. Most of these stocks and sauces can be made in short order, and require no fancy ingredients or techniques.

If you're the thrifty type, save the meaty carcasses from roast chickens, and store them in a big zip-top plastic bag in the freezer to make stock. Bones create a more gelatinous stock when chilled, giving it a savory richness. If you can find them, use chicken backs and wings—even feet—for a less-expensive alternative to a whole bird.

CHICKEN STOCK

HANDS-ON TIME: 12 MIN. TOTAL TIME: 10 HR.

1   (3½-pound) chicken (broiler-fryer)
1   tablespoon black peppercorns
1   teaspoon salt
10 parsley sprigs
6   garlic cloves, sliced
3   bay leaves
2   carrots, cut into 2-inch-thick pieces
1   medium onion, unpeeled and quartered
8   cups water
1   tablespoon cider vinegar (optional)

1. Combine first 8 ingredients in a large Dutch oven; add 8 cups water. Bring to a boil over medium heat. Reduce heat; simmer, uncovered, 40 minutes or until chicken is done.
2. Remove chicken from cooking liquid; cool. Remove meat from bones; reserve for another use. Return bones to cooking liquid; stir in vinegar, if desired. Partially cover and simmer 1 hour.
3. Strain stock through a sieve into a bowl; discard solids. Cover and chill 8 hours. Skim solidified fat from surface; discard.

Note: You can freeze the stock in an airtight container or a zip-top plastic freezer bag for up to 3 months.

SERVES 6 (SERVING SIZE: 1 CUP)
CALORIES 35; FAT 1.3G (SAT 0.4G, MONO 0.5G, POLY 0.3G); PROTEIN 5G; CARB 0G; FIBER 0G; CHOL 16MG; IRON 0MG; SODIUM 405MG; CALC 3MG

simple VEGETABLE STOCK

HANDS-ON TIME: 10 MIN. TOTAL TIME: 1 HR. 10 MIN.

1   whole garlic head
10   cups water
2   cups (1-inch) slices onion
2   cups (1-inch) slices leek
1   cup (1-inch) slices carrot
1   cup (1-inch) slices celery
1   small turnip, peeled and cut into 8 wedges (about ¼ pound)
¼   pound cremini mushrooms, halved
6   black peppercorns
4   parsley sprigs
4   thyme sprigs
1   bay leaf

1. Cut off pointed end of garlic just to expose cloves.
2. Combine garlic and remaining ingredients in a Dutch oven; bring to a boil. Reduce heat, and simmer 50 minutes. Strain through a fine sieve over a bowl; discard solids.

Note: Store the stock in an airtight container in the refrigerator for up to 1 week or in the freezer for up to 1 month.

SERVES 7 (SERVING SIZE: 1 CUP)
CALORIES 6; FAT 0G (SAT 0G, MONO 0G, POLY 0G); PROTEIN 0G; CARB 1G; FIBER 0G; CHOL 0MG; IRON 0MG; SODIUM 4MG; CALC 5MG

classic
CHICKEN NOODLE SOUP

HANDS-ON TIME: 60 MIN. TOTAL TIME: 60 MIN.

With homemade stock in the freezer, you can make this comforting chicken noodle soup whenever you like. Cooking the chicken meat separately keeps it from drying out. White wine sharpens the flavor, and boiling the broth rids it of alcohol so it's fine to serve to kids.

2   tablespoons canola oil
1   bone-in chicken breast half, skinned
1   pound bone-in chicken thighs, skinned
3/4 teaspoon kosher salt, divided
1/2 teaspoon freshly ground black pepper, divided
2   cups chopped onion
1   cup chopped carrot
1/2 cup (1/4-inch-thick) slices celery
1   tablespoon minced fresh garlic
3   parsley sprigs
3   thyme sprigs
1   rosemary sprig
2   bay leaves
1   cup dry white wine
4   cups Chicken Stock (page 240) or unsalted chicken stock
1   cup uncooked medium egg noodles
2   tablespoons chopped fresh parsley

1. Heat a Dutch oven over medium-high heat. Add oil to pan; swirl to coat. Sprinkle chicken with 1/2 teaspoon salt and 1/4 teaspoon pepper. Add chicken, flesh side down. Cook 10 minutes; turn thighs after 5 minutes. Cool; shred. Discard bones.

2. Add onion, carrot, and celery to pan; sauté 10 minutes. Add garlic; sauté 1 minute. Place herb sprigs and bay leaves on cheesecloth. Gather edges; tie securely. Add sachet to pan.

3. Add wine, and bring to a boil. Cook 4 minutes. Add chicken and stock. Cover; reduce heat, and cook 7 minutes.

4. Add noodles; cook 6 minutes or until al dente. Discard sachet. Stir in chopped parsley, 1/4 teaspoon salt, and 1/4 teaspoon pepper.

Note: Store the soup in an airtight container in the refrigerator for up to 3 days.

SERVES 6 (SERVING SIZE: ABOUT 1 CUP)
CALORIES 302; FAT 9.2G (SAT 1.5G, MONO 4.2G, POLY 2.1G); PROTEIN 31G; CARB 16G; FIBER 2G; CHOL 103MG; IRON 2MG; SODIUM 483MG; CALC 54MG

MORE IDEAS

You can thaw some homemade Pasta Dough (page 87) if you have it on hand, roll it out thinly, and cut into shapes with cookie cutters with your kids. You can also cut the dough into thin strips or chop it into bits. Add the noodles a few at a time so they don't stick together, and cook for 1 to 3 minutes.

roasted
BUTTERNUT SOUP

HANDS-ON TIME: 25 MIN. TOTAL TIME: 1 HR. 53 MIN.

A rich orange soup with a hint of sweetness, this recipe uses our homemade vegetable stock with squash that is roasted and pureed for a nutty base. This soup freezes well and is easily doubled. It's a serious crowd-pleaser for company, too.

<table>
<tr><td>1</td><td>(2½-pound) butternut squash</td></tr>
<tr><td colspan="2">Cooking spray</td></tr>
<tr><td>1</td><td>tablespoon extra-virgin olive oil</td></tr>
<tr><td>1½</td><td>cups chopped onion</td></tr>
<tr><td>3</td><td>garlic cloves, minced</td></tr>
<tr><td>6</td><td>cups Simple Vegetable Stock (page 240) or organic vegetable broth</td></tr>
<tr><td>2</td><td>cups coarsely chopped peeled Yukon gold potatoes</td></tr>
<tr><td>2</td><td>teaspoons chopped fresh sage</td></tr>
<tr><td>¾</td><td>teaspoon salt</td></tr>
<tr><td>¼</td><td>teaspoon freshly ground black pepper</td></tr>
<tr><td>1</td><td>bay leaf</td></tr>
<tr><td>2</td><td>tablespoons chopped fresh parsley</td></tr>
<tr><td>2</td><td>teaspoons honey</td></tr>
</table>

1. Preheat oven to 400°.
2. Cut squash in half lengthwise; discard seeds. Place squash, cut sides down, on a foil-lined baking sheet coated with cooking spray. Bake at 400° for 30 minutes or until tender. Cool. Discard peel; mash pulp.
3. Heat a Dutch oven over medium-high heat. Add oil to pan; swirl to coat. Add onion; sauté 4 minutes, stirring occasionally. Add garlic; sauté 30 seconds, stirring constantly. Add squash, stock, and next 5 ingredients (through bay leaf); bring to a boil. Reduce heat, and simmer 45 minutes or until potato is tender, stirring occasionally. Let stand 10 minutes. Discard bay leaf.
4. Place one-third of vegetable mixture in a blender. Remove center piece of blender lid (to allow steam to escape); secure blender lid on blender. Place a clean towel over opening in blender lid (to avoid splatters). Blend until smooth. Pour into a large bowl. Repeat procedure twice with remaining squash mixture. Return pureed mixture to pan; cook over medium heat 3 minutes or until thoroughly heated. Stir in parsley and honey.

Note: Store this in an airtight container in the freezer for up to 2 months.

SERVES 6 (SERVING SIZE: ABOUT 1 CUP)
CALORIES 157; FAT 2.7G (SAT 0.4G, MONO 1.8G, POLY 0.3G); PROTEIN 3G; CARB 33G; FIBER 7G; CHOL 0MG; IRON 1MG; SODIUM 310MG; CALC 83MG

VARIATIONS

Try roasting the squash with cloves of garlic or shallots in the hollows, and then squeeze the roasted garlic into the soup.

Substitute some of the potatoes for carrots or apples for a sweeter soup.

Swap out the herbs for a tablespoon of fresh grated ginger.

quick GRAVY

◇◇

HANDS-ON TIME: 5 MIN. TOTAL TIME: 10 MIN.

◇◇

Cream cheese enriches this lightly meaty gravy with a flour-thickened chicken broth base. It creates a smooth, medium-bodied, herb-flecked sauce. Bring your cream cheese to room temperature before stirring it into the sauce—it blends more smoothly this way, without clumping or curdling. Double or triple the recipe, and freeze.

◇◇

1 cup Chicken Stock (page 240) or unsalted chicken stock, divided
1 tablespoon all-purpose flour
2 tablespoons minced shallots
1 bay leaf
1 tablespoon chopped fresh flat-leaf parsley
2 tablespoons ⅓-less-fat cream cheese, at room temperature
⅛ teaspoon freshly ground black pepper

1. Combine ¼ cup chicken broth and flour in a small saucepan, stirring well with a whisk. Stir in ¾ cup chicken broth, shallots, and bay leaf; bring to a boil.

2. Reduce heat; simmer 3 minutes or until slightly thickened, stirring constantly. Let stand 1 minute; discard bay leaf. Stir in parsley, cheese, and pepper, stirring until cheese melts.

Note: Store the gravy in an airtight container in the refrigerator for up to 5 days.

◇◇

SERVES 4 (SERVING SIZE: ABOUT 3 TABLESPOONS)

CALORIES 38; FAT 1.6G (SAT 1G, MONO 0G, POLY 0G); PROTEIN 2G; CARB 3G; FIBER 0G; CHOL 5MG; IRON 0MG; SODIUM 130MG; CALC 9MG

BÉCHAMEL SAUCE

HANDS-ON TIME: 35 MIN. TOTAL TIME: 35 MIN.

2   tablespoons unsalted butter
¼   cup finely chopped onion
1   tablespoon all-purpose flour
1½   cups whole milk
¼   teaspoon salt
Dash of freshly ground white pepper
Freshly grated nutmeg (optional)

1. Place butter in a small saucepan over medium-low heat; cook until butter melts, stirring occasionally. Add onion to pan; cook 10 minutes or until tender (do not brown), stirring occasionally. Sprinkle flour over onion; cook 2 minutes, stirring occasionally.

2. Gradually add milk to flour mixture, stirring with a whisk until smooth; bring to a simmer. Simmer 10 minutes or until thickened, stirring frequently. Strain mixture through a fine sieve over a bowl; discard solids.

3. Stir in salt, pepper, and nutmeg, if desired. Serve immediately.

Note: You can store the sauce (and the Mornay variation) in an airtight container in the refrigerator for up to 5 days.

SERVES 21 (SERVING SIZE: ABOUT 1 TABLESPOON)

CALORIES 21; FAT 1.6G (SAT 1G, MONO 0.4G, POLY 0.1G); PROTEIN 1G; CARB 1G; FIBER 0G; CHOL 5MG; IRON 0MG; SODIUM 35MG; CALC 20MG

Mornay Sauce

Prepare Béchamel Sauce. Wipe pan clean with paper towels. Return Béchamel Sauce to pan, and place over medium-low heat. Add ½ cup (2 ounces) shredded Gruyère cheese, stirring until smooth. Serve immediately.

SERVES 24 (SERVING SIZE: 1 TABLESPOON)

CALORIES 28; FAT 2.2G (SAT 1.3G, MONO 0.6G, POLY 0.1G); PROTEIN 1G; CARB 1G; FIBER 0G; CHOL 7MG; IRON 0MG; SODIUM 38MG; CALC 40MG

butternut-kale
LASAGNA

HANDS-ON TIME: 15 MIN. TOTAL TIME: 1 HR. 25 MIN.

Gruyère-spiked Mornay sauce drapes the noodles and squash to give this lasagna velvety richness. Hearty, earthy kale balances the sweet squash, and crunchy, toasted pecans top this luscious lasagna. Microwaved precut squash and no-boil lasagna noodles speed up your time in the kitchen.

¼   cup water
1   (12-ounce) package prechopped fresh
     butternut squash
3   cups chopped kale
Cooking spray
1   recipe Mornay Sauce (page 249)
6   no-boil lasagna noodles
1   ounce Gruyère cheese, shredded
3   tablespoons chopped pecans

1. Preheat oven to 450°.
2. Combine ¼ cup water and squash in an 8-inch square glass or ceramic baking dish. Cover tightly with plastic wrap, and pierce plastic wrap 2 to 3 times. Microwave at HIGH 5 minutes or until tender, and drain. Combine squash and kale in a large bowl. Wipe dish dry.
3. Coat baking dish with cooking spray. Spread ⅓ cup Mornay Sauce in bottom of dish. Arrange 2 noodles over sauce; top with half of squash mixture and ⅔ cup sauce. Repeat layers once, ending with remaining noodles and remaining ½ cup sauce. Cover with foil; bake at 450° for 15 minutes. Remove foil; sprinkle Gruyère and pecans over top. Bake, uncovered, at 450° for 10 minutes or until lightly browned and sauce is bubbly. Let stand 5 minutes.

Note: You can store this lasagna in an airtight container for up to 5 days.

SERVES 4 (SERVING SIZE: ¼ OF LASAGNA)
CALORIES 420; FAT 16.3G (SAT 5.8G, MONO 7.3G, POLY 2.1G); PROTEIN 20G; CARB 51G; FIBER 5G; CHOL 29MG; IRON 3MG; SODIUM 556MG; CALC 557MG

VARIATIONS

Other vegetables lend themselves beautifully to this combination of Mornay sauce and pasta. Try cooked chopped spinach with sautéed onions, or a mix of sautéed mushrooms.

mock
HOLLANDAISE

HANDS-ON TIME: 5 MIN. TOTAL TIME: 5 MIN.

Traditional hollandaise sauce is very rich since it's made primarily of butter and egg yolks. This version uses reduced-fat butter-milk and canola mayonnaise to mimic it without going overboard.

⅓   cup reduced-fat buttermilk
⅓   cup canola mayonnaise
½   teaspoon grated lemon rind
1   tablespoon fresh lemon juice
1½   teaspoons Dijon mustard
¼   teaspoon freshly ground black pepper
1½   teaspoons butter

1. Combine first 6 ingredients in a small saucepan over low heat, stirring well with a whisk. Add butter; stir until butter melts. Serve immediately.

Note: This recipe yields ¾ cup sauce.

SERVES 12 (SERVING SIZE: 1 TABLESPOON)

CALORIES 53; FAT 5.5G (SAT 0.8G, MONO 2.8G, POLY 1.4G); PROTEIN 0G; CARB 1G; FIBER 0G; CHOL 4MG; IRON 0MG; SODIUM 64MG; CALC 10MG

crab
EGGS
BENEDICT

HANDS-ON TIME: 10 MIN. TOTAL TIME: 16 MIN.

The chunks of sweet lump crabmeat drenched in creamy egg yolk are a welcome change from the traditional Canadian bacon. Serve with steamed asparagus.

1   tablespoon white wine vinegar
8   large eggs
4   English muffins, toasted
8   ounces fresh lump crabmeat, shell pieces removed
1   recipe Mock Hollandaise
Cracked black pepper
2   tablespoons chopped fresh chives (optional)
1   tablespoon chopped fresh tarragon (optional)

1. Add water to a large skillet, filling two-thirds full. Bring to a boil; reduce heat, and simmer. Add vinegar. Break each egg into a custard cup, and pour gently into pan. Cook 3 minutes or until desired degree of doneness.

2. Place 1 muffin, cut sides up, on each of 4 plates, and divide crab among muffins. Remove eggs from pan using a slotted spoon. Gently place 1 egg on each muffin half. Top each serving with about 3 tablespoons Mock Hollandaise. Sprinkle with cracked pepper. Garnish with chives and tarragon, if desired.

SERVES 4

CALORIES 503; FAT 28.2G (SAT 5.7G, MONO 12.4G, POLY 5.7G); PROTEIN 32G; CARB 30G; FIBER 2G; CHOL 478MG; IRON 5MG; SODIUM 711MG; CALC 127MG

cheddar cheese
SAUCE

HANDS-ON TIME: 10 MIN. TOTAL TIME: 10 MIN.

This mild, kid-friendly sauce gets a subtle tang from sharp cheddar. While slimmed-down, it's still creamy and velvety. It boasts a fraction of the fat you'd find in regular or processed cheese. Stir in the cheese at the end, off the heat, to ensure it doesn't curdle.

1   cup 1% low-fat milk, divided
4   teaspoons all-purpose flour
¼   teaspoon salt
1.5 ounces sharp cheddar cheese, shredded (about ⅓ cup packed)
¼   teaspoon freshly ground black pepper

1. Combine ¼ cup milk and flour in a saucepan; stir with a whisk. Stir in remaining ¾ cup milk and salt; bring to a boil over medium heat, stirring frequently. Reduce heat to low; simmer 2 minutes or until slightly thickened, stirring constantly. Remove from heat. Stir in cheese and pepper, stirring until cheese melts.

Note: This sauce can be stored in an airtight container in the refrigerator for up to 3 days. If the sauce breaks as you're reheating it, gradually whisk in 1 to 2 tablespoons of hot water.

SERVES 8 (SERVING SIZE: 1½ TABLESPOONS)
CALORIES 37; FAT 1.9G (SAT 1.2G, MONO 0.5G, POLY 0.1G); PROTEIN 2G; CARB 3G; FIBER 0G; CHOL 6MG; IRON 0MG; SODIUM 115MG; CALC 71MG

MORE IDEAS

Kids won't be able to resist broccoli or cauliflower smothered in this cheese sauce. It's also delicious spooned over mashed potatoes, stirred into pasta, or served with Chipotle Tortilla Chips (page 194).

slow-cooker
MARINARA

HANDS-ON TIME: 37 MIN. TOTAL TIME: 9 HR. 7 MIN.

Prep the ingredients for this classic tomato sauce the night before, and then let it simmer away while you're at work. Slow cooking concentrates the sweetness and intense tomato essence. You can also use 3 (28-ounce) cans of whole canned tomatoes when tomatoes aren't in season.

- 3 tablespoons extra-virgin olive oil
- 3 cups chopped onion
- ¾ cup diced carrot
- ½ cup diced celery
- ¼ cup minced fresh garlic
- 3 tablespoons chopped fresh oregano
- ¼ teaspoon crushed red pepper
- 2 tablespoons unsalted tomato paste
- ½ cup dry red wine (such as cabernet sauvignon)
- 5½ pounds plum tomatoes, peeled and chopped
- ¾ cup chopped fresh basil
- 1½ teaspoons salt
- ½ teaspoon freshly ground black pepper

1. Heat a large skillet over medium-high heat. Add oil to pan; swirl to coat. Add onion and next 5 ingredients (through red pepper); sauté 8 minutes. Add tomato paste; cook 2 minutes, stirring frequently. Add wine; cook 2 minutes or until liquid almost evaporates.
2. Place vegetable mixture and tomatoes in an electric slow cooker. Cover and cook on LOW 8 hours. Place 3 cups tomato mixture in a blender. Remove center piece of blender lid; secure lid on blender. Place a clean towel over opening in blender lid. Blend until smooth. Return tomato mixture to slow cooker. Add basil, salt, and black pepper. Cook, uncovered, on HIGH 30 minutes.

Note: Store in an airtight container in the refrigerator for up to 2 weeks or in the freezer for up to 3 months.

SERVES 12 (SERVING SIZE: ABOUT ½ CUP)
CALORIES 104; FAT 3.9G (SAT 0.6G, MONO 2.5G, POLY 0.6G); PROTEIN 3G; CARB 15G; FIBER 4G; CHOL 0MG; IRON 1MG; SODIUM 319MG; CALC 51MG

STEP 1

STEP 2

STEP 3

STEP 4

TECHNIQUE

Peeling Tomatoes

1. Make a shallow "X" on the bottom of each tomato.

2. Drop the tomatoes into boiling water for 15 to 20 seconds; remove them with a slotted spoon or tongs.

3. Plunge the tomatoes into ice water. The skins will easily slip off. Remove and discard the skins.

4. Using a small paring knife, cut the core out of the tomato, and then chop.

Italian
TOMATO SOUP

HANDS-ON TIME: 5 MIN. TOTAL TIME: 15 MIN.

Homemade marinara sauce and chicken stock become the base for this easy, kid-friendly soup with tiny tube-shaped pasta and shaved pecorino Romano cheese. Double the recipe, omit the cheese, and freeze some for later.

VARIATIONS

To up the fiber and add more heft to this soup, add a cup of canned chickpeas or kidney beans.

Stir in fresh spinach or chard for extra color and an assortment of nutrients.

Add sliced zucchini or yellow squash for more texture.

3 cups Slow-Cooker Marinara (page 257)
2 cups Chicken Stock (page 240) or unsalted chicken stock
1 cup cooked ditalini pasta
1 ounce shaved fresh pecorino Romano cheese
Basil leaves (optional)

1. Bring marinara and chicken stock to a boil, and stir in pasta. Top soup with shaved pecorino Romano and basil leaves, if desired.

Note: If you're freezing this soup, omit the cheese. The soup will keep in an airtight container or in zip-top plastic freezer bags in the freezer for up to 3 months. Thaw in the refrigerator overnight, and then reheat in the microwave or on the stovetop.

SERVES 4 (SERVING SIZE 1½ CUPS)
CALORIES 242; FAT 8.5G (SAT 2.7G, MONO 3.9G, POLY 1G); PROTEIN 11G; CARB 33G; FIBER 6G; CHOL 8MG; IRON 2MG; SODIUM 682MG; CALC 151MG

PONZU

HANDS-ON TIME: 10 MIN. TOTAL TIME: 10 MIN.

This tangy Japanese dipping sauce has a little heat. If mirin is unavailable, substitute 1 tablespoon rice wine vinegar and 1 tablespoon water or 2 tablespoons dry sherry, and bump up the sugar to 2 teaspoons.

MORE IDEAS

Ponzu is a modern pantry staple. It's often described as a citrus variation of soy, so when you want a dash of lemon juice or soy to amp up flavor in stir-fries and soups, reach for ponzu sauce. In Japanese cooking, it's used as a dip for soba noodles, sashimi, and sometimes dumplings. It's also great in marinades for meat and in vinaigrettes for spicy greens like arugula and kale.

1 tablespoon chopped green onions
3 tablespoons fresh lemon juice
2 tablespoons mirin (sweet rice wine)
2 tablespoons lower-sodium soy sauce
1 teaspoon brown sugar
¼ teaspoon crushed red pepper
¼ teaspoon fish sauce

1. Combine all ingredients in a small bowl; stir with a whisk until sugar dissolves.

Note: Store in an airtight container in the refrigerator for up to 3 days.

SERVES 4 (SERVING SIZE: 2 TABLESPOONS)
CALORIES 30; FAT 0G; PROTEIN 1G; CARB 5G; FIBER 0G; CHOL 0MG; IRON 0MG; SODIUM 225MG; CALC 5MG

spicy
PEANUT DIPPING SAUCE

HANDS-ON TIME: 4 MIN. TOTAL TIME: 4 MIN.

Peanut butter at the dinner table? Yes, please. When mixed with lime, chile, and garlic, it creates a sauce reminiscent of your favorite Thai restaurant. Just combine the ingredients and whisk. One recipe makes enough for a few different meals. Or serve as a dip for raw vegetables.

MORE IDEAS

Double or triple the recipe for this Thai peanut sauce, and use it in many different ways. It is particularly good on grilled meats and baked tofu or as a fabulous pasta sauce with a few Asian vegetables. Top with sprigs of cilantro and rings of green onion. And as a dip, pair it with crunchy cucumber, red peppers, and strips of daikon. Thin it with a little coconut water to use as a salad dressing.

⅓   cup fresh lime juice
1½   tablespoons minced peeled fresh ginger
3   tablespoons water
3   tablespoons lower-sodium soy sauce
3   tablespoons creamy peanut butter
1½   tablespoons honey
2   teaspoons chile paste
3   garlic cloves, minced

1. Combine all ingredients in a small bowl; stir well with a wire whisk.

Note: Store the sauce in an airtight container in the refrigerator for up to 3 days.

SERVES 12 (SERVING SIZE: 1 TABLESPOON)
CALORIES 38; FAT 2G (SAT 0.4G, MONO 1G, POLY 0.6G); PROTEIN 1G; CARB 4G; FIBER 0G; CHOL 0MG; IRON 0MG; SODIUM 209MG; CALC 4MG

NUTRITIONAL INFORMATION

HOW TO USE IT AND WHY

Glance at the end of any *Cooking Light* recipe, and you'll see how committed we are to helping you make the best of today's light cooking. With chefs, registered dietitians, home economists, and a computer system that analyzes every ingredient we use, *Cooking Light* gives you authoritative dietary detail like no other magazine. We go to such lengths so you can see how our recipes fit into your healthful eating plan. If you're trying to lose weight, the calorie and fat figures will probably help most. But if you're keeping a close eye on the sodium, cholesterol, and saturated fat in your diet, we provide those numbers, too. And because many women don't get enough iron or calcium, we can help there, as well. Finally, there's a fiber analysis for those of us who don't get enough roughage.

Here's a helpful guide to put our nutritional analysis numbers into perspective. Remember, one size doesn't fit all, so take your lifestyle, age, and circumstances into consideration when determining your nutrition needs. For example, pregnant or breast-feeding women need more protein, calories, and calcium. And women older than 50 need 1,200mg of calcium daily, 200mg more than the amount recommended for younger women.

IN OUR NUTRITIONAL ANALYSIS, WE USE THESE ABBREVIATIONS

sat	saturated fat	CARB	carbohydrates	g	gram
mono	monounsaturated fat	CHOL	cholesterol	mg	milligram
poly	polyunsaturated fat	CALC	calcium		

DAILY NUTRITION GUIDE

	Women ages 25 to 50	Women over 50	Men ages 24 to 50	Men over 50
Calories	2,000	2,000 or less	2,700	2,500
Protein	50g	50g or less	63g	60g
Fat	65g or less	65g or less	88g or less	83g or less
Saturated Fat	20g or less	20g or less	27g or less	25g or less
Carbohydrates	304g	304g	410g	375g
Fiber	25g to 35g	25g to 35g	25g to 35g	25g to 35g
Cholesterol	300mg or less	300mg or less	300mg or less	300mg or less
Iron	18mg	8mg	8mg	8mg
Sodium	2,300mg or less	1,500mg or less	2,300mg or less	1,500mg or less
Calcium	1,000mg	1,200mg	1,000mg	1,000mg

The nutritional values used in our calculations either come from The Food Processor, Version 10.4 (ESHA Research), or are provided by food manufacturers.

METRIC EQUIVALENTS

The information in the following charts is provided to help cooks outside the United States successfully use the recipes in this book. All equivalents are approximate.

COOKING/OVEN TEMPERATURES

	Fahrenheit	Celsius	Gas Mark
Freeze Water	32° F	0° C	
Room Temp.	68° F	20° C	
Boil Water	212° F	100° C	
Bake	325° F	160° C	3
	350° F	180° C	4
	375° F	190° C	5
	400° F	200° C	6
	425° F	220° C	7
	450° F	230° C	8
Broil			Grill

LIQUID INGREDIENTS BY VOLUME

¼ tsp	=					1 ml	
½ tsp	=					2 ml	
1 tsp	=					5 ml	
3 tsp	=	1 Tbsp	=	½ fl oz	=	15 ml	
2 Tbsp	=	⅛ cup	=	1 fl oz	=	30 ml	
4 Tbsp	=	¼ cup	=	2 fl oz	=	60 ml	
5⅓ Tbsp	=	⅓ cup	=	3 fl oz	=	80 ml	
8 Tbsp	=	½ cup	=	4 fl oz	=	120 ml	
10⅔ Tbsp	=	⅔ cup	=	5 fl oz	=	160 ml	
12 Tbsp	=	¾ cup	=	6 fl oz	=	180 ml	
16 Tbsp	=	1 cup	=	8 fl oz	=	240 ml	
1 pt	=	2 cups	=	16 fl oz	=	480 ml	
1 qt	=	4 cups	=	32 fl oz	=	960 ml	
				33 fl oz	=	1000 ml	= 1 l

DRY INGREDIENTS BY WEIGHT
(To convert ounces to grams, multiply the number of ounces by 30.)

1 oz	=	¹⁄₁₆ lb	=	30 g	
4 oz	=	¼ lb	=	120 g	
8 oz	=	½ lb	=	240 g	
12 oz	=	¾ lb	=	360 g	
16 oz	=	1 lb	=	480 g	

LENGTH
(To convert inches to centimeters, multiply the number of inches by 2.5.)

1 in	=				2.5 cm	
6 in	=	½ ft		=	15 cm	
12 in	=	1 ft		=	30 cm	
36 in	=	3 ft	= 1 yd	=	90 cm	
40 in	=				100 cm	= 1 m

EQUIVALENTS FOR DIFFERENT TYPES OF INGREDIENTS

Standard Cup	Fine Powder (ex. flour)	Grain (ex. rice)	Granular (ex. sugar)	Liquid Solids (ex. butter)	Liquid (ex. milk)
1	140 g	150 g	190 g	200 g	240 ml
¾	105 g	113 g	143 g	150 g	180 ml
⅔	93 g	100 g	125 g	133 g	160 ml
½	70 g	75 g	95 g	100 g	120 ml
⅓	47 g	50 g	63 g	67 g	80 ml
¼	35 g	38 g	48 g	50 g	60 ml
⅛	18 g	19 g	24 g	25 g	30 ml

RECItPE INDEX

A

Almond Butter, 160
Apple Hand Pies, Spiced, 66
Apricot-Fig Chutney, 150

B

Bacon Vinaigrette, Sweet-
and-Sour, 185
Banana-Muesli Muffins, 51
Banana Pancakes, Peanut
Butter and, 25
Beverage Mixes
Chai Tea Mix, 236
Spiced Mocha Mix, 235
Biscuits
Buttermilk Biscuits, 37
Herbed Asiago Biscuits, 38
Mix, Biscuit, 37
Sweet Potato Biscuits with
Honey-Pecan Butter, 41
Blueberries
Muffins, Blueberry, 44
Pancakes, Gluten-Free
Blueberry-Almond
Oatmeal, 33
Pies, Blueberry Hand, 66
Breads. *See also* specific
types.
Breadsticks, Cheesy
Herb, 82
Scones, Chocolate-
Cherry, 43
Yeast
Focaccia, Fig and
Onion, 102

Honey Whole-Wheat
Bread, 99
Whole-Wheat Pita
Bread, 105
Butter
Almond Butter, 160
Cashew Butter, 160
Hazelnut Butter, 163
Honey-Pecan Butter, Sweet
Potato Biscuits with, 41
Macadamia Butter, 162
Nut Butters, Homemade, 160
Peanut Butter, 160
Pecan Butter, 162
Pistachio Butter, 163
Walnut Butter, 160

C

Calzones, Spinach and
Mushroom, 81
Cashew Butter, 160
Cereal
Breakfast Cereal, 49
Muesli with Cranberries and
Flaxseed, 49
Cheese
Crackers, Cheddar Cheese
Snack, 203
Crackers, Parmesan-
Rosemary Flatbread,
206
Homemade
Mozzarella, Homemade,
120
Queso Fresco, Homemade,
128

Ricotta Cheese,
Homemade, 132
Sauce, Cheddar Cheese, 255
Sauce, Mornay, 249
Torte with Fresh Berry
Topping, Ricotta, 135
Cherry Pie Bars, 220
Chicken
Buns, Steamed Curried
Chicken, 84
Pita, Chicken-Tzatziki, 106
Soup, Classic Chicken
Noodle, 243
Stock, Chicken, 240
Tacos with Pineapple Slaw,
BBQ Chicken Soft, 113
Tacos with Spicy Ranchero
Sauce and Cilantro Slaw,
Smoked Chicken, 111
Chips
Chipotle Tortilla Chips, 194
Microwave Sweet Potato
Chips, 191
Pita Chips, 192
Plantain Chips, 197
Potato Chips, Crispy, 191
Tortilla Chips, Nacho
Cheese, 188
Chutney, Apricot-Fig, 150
Chutney, Red Tomato, 153
Cookies
Bars
Cherry Pie Bars, 220
Chocolate–Pecan Pie
Bars, 220
Oatmeal-Raisin Bars, 220
Quinoa-Granola Chocolate

Chip Cookies, 55
Refrigerator
  Chocolate Crème-Filled
    Sandwich Cookies, 214
  Chocolate-Espresso
    Cookies, 71
  Cranberry-Orange
    Cookies, 71
  Peanut Butter Sandwich
    Cookies, 217
  Spiced Molasses
    Cookies, 71
  Vanilla Slice-and-Bake
    Cookies, 71
Corn Tortillas, 108
Crab Eggs Benedict, 252
Crackers
  Cheddar Cheese Snack
    Crackers, 203
  Graham Crackers, 199
  Honey-Wheat Buttery
    Crackers, 200
  Nutty Whole-Grain
    Crackers, 205
  Parmesan-Rosemary
    Flatbread Crackers, 206
Cranberry
  Cookies, Cranberry-
    Orange, 71
  Muesli with Cranberries and
    Flaxseed, 49
  Sauce, Basic Cranberry, 156

D

Desserts. *See also* Cookies;
  Doughnuts; Ice Cream;
  Pies and Pastries.
  Marshmallows,
    Chocolate, 213

Tacos with Ice Cream and
  Peanuts, Chocolate, 138
Dip, Creamy Ranch-Style, 230
Dip, Sour Cream and
  Onion, 232
Dough
  Pasta Dough, Classic, 87
  Pizza Dough, 76
  Pizza Dough, Whole-
    Wheat, 76
Doughnuts
  Baked Doughnuts,
    Homemade, 72
  Chocolate-Glazed
    Doughnuts, 72
  Cinnamon-Glazed
    Doughnuts, 72

E

Eggs Benedict, Crab, 252

F

Figs
  Baked Figs, Granola with
    Honeyed Yogurt and,
    119
  Chutney, Apricot-Fig, 150
  Focaccia, Fig and Onion,
    102
  Toaster Pastries with
    Lemon Glaze, Fig, 69
  Filling, Ravioli with Herbed
    Ricotta, 89
  Flatbread Crackers, Parmesan-
    Rosemary, 206
  Flatbread with Pesto,
    Mozzarella, Tomato, and
    Arugula, 125

French Toast Sandwiches,
  Chocolate-Hazelnut, 166
Fruit. *See also* specific types.
  Compote, Citrusy Ginger-
    Flax Waffles with Mixed
    Berry, 28
  Compote, Warm Berry, 155
  Leather, Peach-Strawberry
    Fruit, 223
  Topping, Ricotta Torte with
    Fresh Berry, 135

G

Glaze, Cinnamon–Brown
  Sugar Toaster Pastries
  with Cinnamon, 69
Glaze, Fig Toaster Pastries
  with Lemon, 69
Gnocchi and Arugula with
  Lemon-Thyme Butter
  Sauce, 93
Gnocchi, Homemade, 90
Granola
  Cookies, Quinoa-Granola
    Chocolate Chip, 55
  Honeyed Yogurt and Baked
    Figs, Granola with, 119
  Nutty Whole-Grain
    Granola, 52
  Squares, No-Bake PB–
    Chocolate Chip
    Granola, 218
  Sunflower Granola, 57
  Sunflower Granola
    Breakfast Parfaits, 57
Grape Jam, Concord, 144
Gravy, Quick, 246

H

Hazelnut Butter, 163
Hazelnut Spread,
    Chocolate-, 165
Hummus
    Feta-Baked Hummus, 229
    Spicy Red Pepper
        Hummus, 229
    Traditional Hummus, 229

I

Ice Cream, Chocolate Fudge
    Brownie, 141
Ice Cream, Vanilla Bean, 136

J

Jam, Concord Grape, 144
Jam, Fresh Strawberry, 147

L

Lasagna, Butternut-Kale, 251
Lemon Curd, 148
Linguine, Spinach-Herb
    Pesto, 171

M

Macadamia Butter, 162
Marmalade, Caramelized
    Onion, 159
Marshmallows, Chocolate, 213
Mayonnaise, Homemade, 176
Meatball Subs, 127

Mixes
Baking
    Gluten-Free Oatmeal
        Pancake and Waffle
        Mix, 31
    Muffin Mix, 44
    Pancake and Waffle
        Mix, 23
    Chai Tea Mix, 236
    Spiced Mocha Mix, 235
Muesli
    Breakfast Cereal, 49
    Cranberries and Flaxseed,
        Muesli with, 49
Muffins
    Banana-Muesli Muffins, 51
    Blueberry Muffins, 44
    Double Chocolate
        Muffins, 46
    Mix, Muffin, 44
    Mushroom Calzones, Spinach
        and, 81
Mustard
    Grainy Mustard, 173
    Homemade Basic
        Mustard, 173
    Honey Mustard, 173

N

Nuts. *See also* specific types.
    Butters, Homemade
        Nut, 160
    Granola, Nutty Whole-
        Grain, 52

O

Oats
    Bars, Oatmeal-Raisin, 220

Pancakes, Gluten-Free
    Oatmeal, 31
Waffles, Gluten-Free Pecan-
    Oatmeal, 34
Onions
    Caramelized Onion
        Marmalade, 159
    Dip, Sour Cream and
        Onion, 232
    Focaccia, Fig and Onion, 102

P

Pancakes
    Buttermilk Pancakes, 23
    Gluten-Free Blueberry-
        Almond Oatmeal
        Pancakes, 33
    Gluten-Free Oatmeal
        Pancakes, 31
    Mix, Gluten-Free Oatmeal
        Pancake and Waffle, 31
    Mix, Pancake and Waffle, 23
    Peanut Butter and Banana
        Pancakes, 25
Pasta. *See also* Lasagna;
    Ravioli.
    Dough, Classic Pasta, 87
    Linguine, Spinach-Herb
        Pesto, 171
Peach Pie with Ginger-Pecan
    Streusel, 63
Peach-Strawberry Fruit
    Leather, 223
Peanut
    Butter, Peanut, 160
    Caramel Corn, Peanut
        Butter, 211
    Chocolate Tacos with Ice
        Cream and Peanuts, 138

Cookies, Peanut Butter Sandwich, 217

Granola Squares, No-Bake PB–Chocolate Chip, 218

Pancakes, Peanut Butter and Banana, 25

Sauce, Spicy Peanut Dipping, 262

Pecans

Bars, Chocolate–Pecan Pie, 220

Butter, Pecan, 160

Butter, Sweet Potato Biscuits with Honey-Pecan, 41

Streusel, Peach Pie with Ginger-Pecan, 63

Waffles, Gluten-Free Pecan-Oatmeal, 34

Peppers

Chipotle Tortilla Chips, 194

Hatch Chile Salsa, Roasted, 225

Red Pepper Hummus, Spicy, 229

Salsa Verde, 226

Pesto, 168

Pesto Linguine, Spinach-Herb, 171

Pies and Pastries

Crust, Homemade Pie, 60

Hand Pies, Blueberry, 66

Hand Pies, Spiced Apple, 66

Peach Pie with Ginger-Pecan Streusel, 63

Tart, Tomato-Ricotta, 64

Toaster Pastries, Strawberry, 69

Toaster Pastries with Cinna-mon Glaze, Cinnamon–Brown Sugar, 69

Toaster Pastries with Lemon Glaze, Fig, 69

Pistachio Butter, 163

Pita Chips, 192

Pizza

Dough, Pizza, 76

Dough, Whole-Wheat Pizza, 76

Roasted Vegetable and Ricotta Pizza, 79

Plantain Chips, 197

Ponzu, 260

Popcorn

Lemon-Parmesan Popcorn, 208

Peanut Butter Caramel Corn, 211

Potatoes

Biscuits with Honey-Pecan Butter, Sweet Potato, 41

Chips, Crispy Potato, 191

Chips, Microwave Sweet Potato, 191

R

Ravioli with Herbed Ricotta Filling, 89

Rolls and Buns

Cinnamon Rolls with Dates, 75

Steamed Curried Chicken Buns, 84

Whole-Wheat Hamburger Buns, 94

S

Salads and Salad Dressings

Caprese "Salsa" Zucchini with Sea Salt, 122

Dressing, Four-Herb Green Goddess, 183

Slaw, BBQ Chicken Soft Tacos with Pineapple, 113

Slaw, Smoked Chicken Tacos with Spicy Ranchero Sauce and Cilantro, 111

Vinaigrette, Sweet-and-Sour Bacon, 185

Vinaigrette, Tomato-Basil, 185

Salsa, Roasted Hatch Chile, 225

Salsa Verde, 226

Sandwiches

Burgers, Thai Turkey, 96

Calzones, Spinach and Mushroom, 81

French Toast Sandwiches, Chocolate-Hazelnut, 166

Melt, Turkey-Apple-Gouda, 101

Pita, Chicken-Tzatziki, 106

Subs, Meatball, 127

Sauces. *See also* Gravy; Pesto; Salsa; Toppings.

Béchamel Sauce, 249

Cheddar Cheese Sauce, 255

Cranberry Sauce, Basic, 156

Lemon-Thyme Butter Sauce, Gnocchi and Arugula with, 93

Marinara, Slow-Cooker, 257

Memphis Barbecue Sauce, 179

Mock Hollandaise, 252
Mornay Sauce, 249
Ponzu, 260
Spicy Peanut Dipping
    Sauce, 262
Spicy Ranchero Sauce and
    Cilantro Slaw, Smoked
    Chicken Tacos with, 111
Tartar Sauce, 176
Tzatziki, 116
White BBQ Sauce, 180
Scones, Chocolate-Cherry, 43
Shrimp Tacos, Blackened, 131
Slow-Cooker Marinara, 257
Snacks. *See also* Chips;
    Crackers; Dip; Granola;
    Hummus.
Caramel Corn, Peanut
    Butter, 211
Fruit Leather, Peach-
    Strawberry, 223
Marshmallows,
    Chocolate, 213
Popcorn, Lemon-
    Parmesan, 208
Soups and Stocks
Chicken Noodle Soup,
    Classic, 243
Roasted Butternut
    Soup, 244
Stock, Chicken, 240
Stock, Simple
    Vegetable, 240
Tomato Soup, Italian, 258
Spinach and Mushroom
    Calzones, 81
Spinach-Herb Pesto
    Linguine, 171

Spread. *See also* Butter; Jam;
    Marmalade; Mayonnaise;
    Mustard.
Chocolate-Hazelnut
    Spread, 165
Squash
Butternut-Kale Lasagna, 251
Butternut Soup,
    Roasted, 244
Zucchini with Sea Salt,
    Caprese "Salsa," 122
Strawberries
Fruit Leather, Peach-
    Strawberry, 223
Jam, Fresh Strawberry, 147
Toaster Pastries, Straw-
    berry, 69
Sunflower Granola, 57
Sunflower Granola Breakfast
    Parfaits, 57

T

Tacos
BBQ Chicken Soft Tacos
    with Pineapple Slaw, 113
Blackened Shrimp Tacos,
    131
Chocolate Tacos with Ice
    Cream and Peanuts, 138
Smoked Chicken Tacos with
    Spicy Ranchero Sauce
    and Cilantro Slaw, 111
Technique
Caramelizing Onions, 159
Forming Graham Crackers,
    199
How to Cut Nutty Whole-
    Grain Crackers, 205
Kneading Pizza Dough, 76

Making Chocolate Taco
    Shells, 138
Making Compound
    Butter, 41
Making Fruit Leather, 223
Making Mayonnaise, 176
Making Pie Crust, 60
Making Queso Fresco, 128
Making Ricotta, 132
Making the Best Biscuits, 38
Making the Best Muffins, 46
Peeling Tomatoes, 257
Properly Peaked, 28
Shaping Calzones, 81
Shaping Hand Pies, 66
Shaping Pasta, 87
Shaping Steamed Buns, 84
Tomatoes
Chutney, Red Tomato, 153
Ketchup, Heirloom
    Tomato, 174
Marinara, Slow-Cooker, 257
Soup, Italian Tomato, 258
Tart, Tomato-Ricotta, 64
Vinaigrette, Tomato-
    Basil, 185
Toppings. *See also* Glaze;
    Sauces.
Heirloom Tomato Ketchup,
    174
Sweet
Fresh Berry Topping,
    Ricotta Torte with, 135
Ginger-Pecan Streusel,
    Peach Pie with, 63
Lemon Curd, 148
Tortillas
Chips, Chipotle Tortilla, 194
Chips, Nacho Cheese
    Tortilla, 188

Corn Tortillas, 108
Flour Tortillas, 108
Turkey-Apple-Gouda Melt, 101
Turkey Burgers, Thai, 96
Tzatziki, 116
Tzatziki Pita, Chicken-, 106

Vegetables. *See also* specific
    types.
  Pizza, Roasted Vegetable
    and Ricotta, 79

Stock, Simple
    Vegetable, 240

Waffles
  Buttermilk Belgian
    Waffles, 26
  Ginger-Flax Waffles with
    Mixed Berry Compote,
    Citrusy, 28
  Gluten-Free Pecan-Oatmeal
    Waffles, 34

Mix, Gluten-Free Oatmeal
    Pancake and Waffle, 31
  Mix, Pancake and Waffle, 23
Walnut Butter, 160

Yogurt, Homemade, 116

SUBJECT INDEX

food safety when freezing, 18
How Long Does Food Last?
    (chart), 19
  in the freezer, 19
  in the fridge, 19
  in the pantry, 19
Organizing Your Pantry, 11
  consider placement of food
    in fridge, 11
  create zones for groups of
    food, 11
  label and date foods
    clearly, 11

oils, determining freshness
    of, 11
spices, determining fresh-
    ness of, 11
Smart Freezer Storage, 17–18
  Best Foods to Freeze, 18
  freezing fruits, 17
  freezing herbs, 18
  freezing vegetables, 17
  Tips for Effective
    Freezing, 18
    containers to use, 18
    food safety, 18

keep freezer full, 18
  keep freezer organized, 18
Smart Shopping Tips, 14
  get your money's worth
    when buying non-
    perishables, canned
    foods, or dry goods, 14
Stocking Your Pantry, 13
  list of staples and place-
    ment of in the
    kitchen, 13

ISBN-13: 978-0-8487-4397-0
ISBN-10: 0-8487-4397-0
Library of Congress Control Number: 2015931552

Printed in the United States of America
First Printing 2015

Oxmoor House
Editorial Director: Anja Schmidt
Creative Director: Felicity Keane
Art Director: Christopher Rhoads
Executive Photography Director: Iain Bagwell
Executive Food Director: Grace Parisi
Photo Editor: Kellie Lindsey
Managing Editor: Elizabeth Tyler Austin
Assistant Managing Editor: Jeanne de Lathouder

Cooking Light The Good Pantry
Senior Editor: Betty Wong
Editor: Rachel Quinlivan West, R.D.
Project Editor: Sarah Waller
Editorial Assistant: April Smitherman
Assistant Designer: Allison Sperando Potter
Assistant Test Kitchen Manager: Alyson Moreland Haynes
Recipe Developers and Testers: Stefanie Maloney; Callie Nash; Karen Rankin
Food Stylists: Nathan Carrabba, Victoria E. Cox, Margaret Monroe Dickey, Catherine Crowell Steele
Senior Photographer: Hélène Dujardin
Senior Photo Stylists: Kay E. Clarke, Mindi Shapiro Levine
Associate Production Manager: Kimberly Marshall
Assistant Production Manager: Diane Rose Keener

Contributors
Writer: Dianne Jacob
Designer: Alissa Faden
Copy Editors: Jacqueline Giovanelli, Deri Reed
Proofreader: Julie Bosche
Indexer: Mary Ann Laurens
Photographers: Jim Bathie, Beau Gustafson, Becky Luigart-Stayner
Photo Stylists: Cindy Barr, Mary Clayton Carl, Missie Neville Crawford, Leslie Simpson
Food Stylists: Tami Hardeman, Erica Hopper, Ana Price Kelly
Recipe Developers and Testers: Tamara Goldis, R.D., Wendy Treadwell, R.D., Leah Van Deren
Fellows: Laura Arnold, Kylie Dazzo, Nicole Fisher, Elizabeth Laseter, Loren Lorenzo, Anna Ramia, Caroline Smith, Amanda Widis

Time Inc. Books
Publisher: Margot Schupf
Vice President, Finance: Vandana Patel
Executive Director, Marketing Services: Carol Pittard
Executive Director, Business Development: Suzanne Albert
Executive Director, Marketing: Susan Hettleman
Assistant General Counsel: Simone Procas
Assistant Project Manager: Allyson Angle

Wood letters on cover created by madfish designs